Nita Mehta's

GREAT
INDIAN
COOKING

VEGETARIAN

Nita Mehta

B.Sc. (Home Science), M.Sc. (Food and Nutrition), Gold Medalist

Co-Author:

Tanya Mehta

SNAB
Excellence in Books

Snab Publishers Pvt Ltd

Corporate Office
3A/3, Asaf Ali Road, New Delhi 110 002
Phone: +91 11 2325 2948, 2325 0091
Telefax: +91 11 2325 0091
E-mail: nitamehta@nitamehta.com
Website: www.nitamehta.com

Editorial and Marketing office
E-159, Greater Kailash II, New Delhi 110 048

Food Styling and Photography by Snab
Typesetting by National Information Technology Academy
3A/3, Asaf Ali Road, New Delhi 110 002

Recipe Development & Testing:
Nita Mehta Foods - R & D Centre
3A/3, Asaf Ali Road, New Delhi - 110002
E-143, Amar Colony, Lajpat Nagar-IV, New Delhi - 110024

Distributed by :
NITA MEHTA BOOKS
3A/3, Asaf Ali Road, New Delhi - 02
Distribution Centre :
D16/1, Okhla Industrial Area, Phase-I,
New Delhi - 110020
Tel.: 26813199, 26813200
E-mail: nitamehta.mehta@gmail.com

Contributing Writers :
Anurag Mehta
Tanya Mehta
Subhash Mehta

Editors :
Sangeeta
Sunita

ISBN 978-81-7869-051-3
First Print 2012
Cover designed by: flyingtrees

Printed in India at Aegean Offset Printers, Greater Noida

Price: Rs. 295/-

Introduction

In India, cooking is a way of expressing love. Indian food is not just a blend of spices and condiments but the food is cooked carefully, adding the right spice, the right amount of spice and at the right time. Here is a book with great recipes which will take care of all this.

Indian cuisine is very broadly divided into North Indian cuisine and South Indian cuisine. We have included the fiery South Indian Rasam, Idli, Bisi Bele Bhath, Avial - the South Indian mixed vegetable, and many others. The Kashmiri Dum Aloo, Khumb Matar Miloni, Bharwaan Kofte are some of the contributions from North India.

This book offers even Indian drinks and soups besides the regular meals. The classic Thandai and Ambi Panna are now made more delicious. There are new creations like Anjeeri Khushboo. Anjeer (Fig) is considered to be a very healthy fruit and is abundantly available too. Indian soups may sound a little weird but the peppery Mulligatawny Soup originated in the South of India. Shorbas are thin soups which are tempered with Indian spices. A section on Chutneys and Raitas makes the book complete.

Pulses and lentils (Dals) form an important source of proteins for a vegetarian Indian meal. A simple dal can turn into an exotic one with just a different flavouring. At the same time, if not well prepared, dal can be very boring! The book explains very clearly, how to flavour your pulses the right way!

The vegetables are eaten with rice or Indian breads (roti). Exotic biryaanis and pulaos prepared from Indian basmati rice, flavoured with magical spices like fennel seeds, cinnamon sticks and cardamom pods, are all explained simply. The Indian flat breads - nan, phulka and paranthas are just wonderful! The book tells you, how just a few black sesame seeds and shredded almonds add that special touch to the simple nans, making them exotic!

Special Indian sweets have been included. The Indian Ice Cream - Kulfi is our speciality. Enjoy all this and many more delights of Indian food. Happy Cooking!

Nita Mehta

Contents

Herbs & Spices

Asafoetida
(Hing)

Bay Leaves
(Tej Patta)

Cardamom
(Chhoti Elaichi)

Cardamom, Black
(Moti Elaichi)

Carom Seeds
(Ajwain)

Green Chillies
(Hari Mirch)

Dry Red Chilli
(Sukhi Saboot Lal Mirch)

Red Chilli Powder
(Lal Mirch Powder)

Cinnamon
(dalchini)

Cloves
(Laung)

Coriander Seeds
(Saboot Dhania)

Coriander Seeds Ground
(Dhania Powder)

Coriander Leaves
(Hara Dhania)

Cumin Seeds
(Jeera)

Black Cumin Seeds
(Shah Jeera)

Curry Leaves
(Kari Patta)

Fennel Seeds (Saunf)

Fenugreek Seeds (Methi Dana)

Fenugreek Leaves, Dried (Kasoori Methi)

Garam Masala Powder (Garam Masala)

Garlic (Lahsun)

Ginger (Adrak)

Mace (Javitri)

Mango Powder, Dried (Amchoor)

Melon Seeds (Magaz)

Mint Leaves (Pudina)

Mustard Seed (Sarson)

Nigella, Onion Seeds (Kalaunji)

Nutmeg (Jaiphal)

Peppercorns (Sabut Kali Mirch)

Pomegranate Seeds, Dried (Anardana)

Sesame Seeds (Til)

Saffron (Kesar)

Turmeric Powder (Haldi)

Brown Mustard Seed (Rai)

Poppy Seeds (Khus-Khus)

Home made Indian Spice Blends

To perk up the flavour of Indian dishes.

GARAM MASALA

Makes ¼ cup

2" sticks cinnamon (*dalchini*) - 5-6
15-20 black cardamom pods (*moti elaichi*)
¾ tbsp cloves (*laung*)
2 tbsp black peppercorns (*saboot kali mirch*)
2 tbsp cumin seeds (*jeera*)
½ flower of mace (*javitri*)

1. Remove seeds of black cardamoms. Discard skin.
2. Roast all ingredients together in a skillet for 2 minutes on low heat, stirring constantly, till fragrant.
3. Remove from heat. Cool. Grind to a fine powder in a clean coffee or spice grinder. Store in a small jar with a tight fitting lid.

CHAAT MASALA

Makes ¾ cup

3 tbsp cumin seeds (*jeera*)
1 tbsp ground ginger (*sonth*)
2 tsp carom seeds (*ajwain*)
2 tsp raw mango powder (*amchoor*)
2 tbsp ground black salt (*kala namak*)
1 tsp salt, 1 tsp ground black pepper
½ tsp ground nutmeg (*jaiphal*)

1. Roast cumin seeds in a small nonstick skillet or a wok to a golden brown colour. Transfer to a bowl and set aside.
2. Roast carom seeds over moderate heat for about 2 minutes, till fragrant.
3. Grind roasted cumin seeds & carom seeds. Mix in the remaining ingredients.
4. Store in an air-tight jar.

TANDOORI MASALA

Makes ½ cup

2 tbsp coriander seeds (*saboot dhania*)
2 tbsp cumin seeds (*jeera*)
1 tsp fenugreek seeds (*methi daana*)
1 tbsp black peppercorns
1 tbsp cloves (*laung*)
seeds of 8 black cardamom pods
2 tsp paprika (*degi mirch*)
1 tbsp dried fenugreek leaves
1 tbsp ground cinnamon (*dalchini*)
½ tbsp ground ginger (*sonth*)
½ tsp red chilli powder

1. In a non-stick skillet, roast together - coriander seeds, cumin seeds, fenugreek seeds, black peppercorns, cloves and cardamom seeds, on moderate heat for about 1 minute, until fragrant.

2. Remove from heat and let the spices cool down. Grind to a fine powder. Transfer to a bowl and mix in the remaining ingredients. Store in an air tight jar.

SAMBHAR POWDER

Makes ½ cup

¼ cup coriander seeds (*saboot dhania*)
1 tbsp cumin seeds (*jeera*)
1 tbsp dried, split yellow chick peas
(*channe ki dal*)
2 tsp fenugreek seeds (*methi daana*)
5-6 dry, red chillies (*saboot lal mirch*)
½ tsp asafoetida (*hing*)
1½ tsp peppercorns (*saboot kali mirch*)

1. Roast all ingredients together over low heat in a nonstick skillet, until fragrant.

2. Cool the spices and grind to a fine powder in a small coffee grinder. Store in an air tight jar.

The Indian Spice Box

Almost every Indian kitchen has this box with various compartments to hold the basic spices and salt.

- Ground Coriander Seeds (*dhania* powder)
- Cumin Seeds (*jeera*)
- Salt
- Dried Mango Powder (*amchoor*)
- Turmeric (*haldi*)
- Garam Masala
- Red Chilli Powder (*laal mirch* powder)

Some Cooking Utensils

KADHAI (WOK) - The kadhai is a deep pan, round bottomed with two handles on the sides. Used mainly for frying and making Indian masala dishes. When buying one, choose a heavy-bottomed one in a medium size. Steel/Brass kadhais were used earlier, but now aluminium or non-stick ones are more popular. Copper-bottomed metal kadhais are also becoming popular.

SAUCE PAN - These are deep pans with a handle. Useful for making tea, blanching vegetables in water or working with food where some sauce is needed. Usually these are made of stainless steel and are available in various sizes. Nonstick ones are also available.

PATILA (DEEP METAL PANS) - Used for boiling water, milk, rice, pasta etc. Buy a heavy-bottom one. Deep non-stick pots with handles are also available which are very handy for making soups, rice and curries.

TAWA (GRIDDLE) - A heavy iron tawa makes good chappatis. Buy one with a handle. These days non stick griddles are also available.

NON STICK FRYING PAN (SAUTE PAN, SKILLET) - A pan about 2" high is ideal for shallow frying tikkis, kebabs and other snacks. It makes a good utensil for cooking dry/semi dry dishes too. The vegetables lie flat in a single layer on the wide bottom making them crunchy on the outside and yet moist from inside. Remember to use a plastic or a wooden spoon/spatula to stir and fry in all nonstick vessels. Metallic ones will scratch the non stick finish and ruin it. Avoid strong detergents for washing them, warm soapy water is best. It is good to have one small (about 7" diameter) and one big (10 " diameter) pan. Pancakes too can be made conveniently in them.

CHAKLA-BELAN (ROLLING BOARD-ROLLING PIN) - A marble or heavy weight rolling board is ideal for rolling out dough for chapatis, poori etc. A wooden rolling pin with it makes the set complete. Plastic rolling pins are available but I am not too comfortable with them.

PARAT (SHALLOW BOWL TO KNEAD DOUGH) - Shallow bowl to make dough, generally stainless steel. Buy a medium size even if you are a small family, because if the bowl is too small, the surrounding area tends to get messy while making the dough. Dough can also be made in a food processor.

KADCCHI (LADLE) - Large, long - handled spoon with a small shallow bowl like spoon at the end. Should be strong enough for stirring masalas.

CHHANNI (LARGE STEEL COLANDER)

A big, wide strainer with large holes for draining cooked rice, pasta and for draining fresh vegetables after washing.

PALTA (PANCAKE TURNER) - These broad metal turners have thin, flexible yet sturdy blade that will slide easily under the food and then be strong enough to turn the food. Not just for pancakes, it's great for turning kebabs too. Ideally choose one with a heat-resistant handle.

CHHARA, PAUNI (SLOTTED SPOON) - A big round, flat spoon with holes and a long handle. Good for removing fried food from oil as it drains out the oil nicely through the holes. Also used to lift solid foods out of cooking liquids.

Drinks

drinks

Minty Ambi Panna

The sweet and sour Indian cooler prepared from raw mangoes.

Serves 6-8

½ kg raw green mangoes, ¾ cup sugar, ½ cup mint leaves (*poodina*)
2 tsp roasted cumin (*bhuna jeera*) powder, 2 tsp salt, a mint sprig - for garnish

1. Peel raw mangoes. Discard skin.
2. Place peeled mangoes in a pressure cooker with 6 cups of water and pressure cook to give 2-3 whistles. Remove from heat.
3. When cool, extract the pulp of the mangoes with the hands and discard the seeds. Mix the pulp and water in the pressure cooker well.
4. Blend the mint leaves to a smooth paste by adding a little water.
5. Add mint, cumin powder, powdered sugar (or can add granulated sugar when the mixture is slightly warm, it will dissolve easily) and salt. Mix well.
6. Take a muslin cloth or a very fine metal strainer and strain the mixture. Check and adjust the seasonings as a lot depends on the sourness of the mangoes. Chill.
7. Pour the panna over ice put in glasses and garnish with a mint sprig.

Thandai

A festive drink prepared from nuts and flavourful spices blended in milk.

Serves 6-8

8 cups milk (1½ litres), 10-12 tbsp sugar, ½ cup almonds (30 pieces, about 4-5 per glass)
¼ cup + 2 tbsp seeds of watermelon (*magaz*), 8 tbsp poppy seeds (*khus khus*)
2 tbsp broken cashewnuts (*kaju*), 15-20 peppercorns (*saboot kali mirch*)
6-8 green cardamoms (*chhoti elaichi*), few dried rose petals
a few strands of saffron (*kesar*) - soaked in warm water for garnishing

1. Soak almonds separately in water for 3-4 hours.

2. Soak together- watermelon seeds, poppy seeds, cashewnuts, peppercorns, green cardamoms and rose petals for 3-4 hours. Strain.

3. Peel the almonds and add to the other ingredients. Put all the soaked ingredients in a mixer grinder and grind to a smooth paste by adding a little water or milk. The grinding of the ingredients should be done very well. Grind well 3-4 times to extract the juices as well as the flavour by adding some water or milk.

4. Add the ground ingredients to the milk. Add sugar and mix well.

5. Strain the milk through a muslin cloth and discard the residue.

6. Chill the thandai by adding ice. Serve garnished with soaked saffron.

Gulab ka Soda Sherbet

Serves 4

¾ cup rose syrup or *sherbat*
500 ml soda water - chilled, 4-5 tsp lemon juice
¼ tsp pepper, ½ tsp salt, ¼ tsp black salt (*kala namak*)
a lemon slice and a mint sprig - for garnish

1. Mix rose syrup or *sherbat*, lemon juice, pepper, salt and black salt in a large pan. Keep aside till serving time.

2. To serve, fill ¼ of each glass with ice cubes or crushed ice.

3. Pour soda in the rose mixture in the pan.

4. Pour the prepared rose cooler into the glasses. Garnish with a lemon slice and a mint sprig. Serve immediately.

Anjeeri Khushboo

A delicious drink.

Serves 5-6

10-12 dried figs (*anjeer*)
½ tsp saffron (*kesar*)
6-7 tbsp honey
5 cups chilled milk (1 litre)
1 small cup (100 ml) vanilla ice cream
10-12 strands of saffron - soaked in 1 tsp water for sometime, for garnish

1. Soak figs in warm water for ½ hour and chop finely.

2. Soak saffron in 3-4 tbsp of warm milk.

3. In a blender, put chilled milk, chopped figs, honey, ice cream, saffron and 2-3 cubes of ice. Blend well till smooth and frothy.

4. Pour the shake in individual glasses. Garnish with 1-2 strands of soaked saffron.

Imli Jeera Paani

Serves 4

4 cups water
1 rounded tbsp seedless tamarind or tamarind pulp, 4 tsp lemon juice, 1 tbsp sugar
½ tsp black salt (*kala namak*), 1½ tsp roasted cumin (*bhuna jeera*) powder
¾ tsp salt, or to taste, 1 bunch of mint leaves and 1" piece ginger - ground to a paste
2 tbsp *besan ki pakories* or *boondi* (*raite waali pakories*)

1. Soak tamarind in 1 cup hot water. Extract pulp. Strain the pulp.
2. Grind mint leaves and ginger with a little water to a smooth paste.
3. Add mint leaves paste to tamarind water.
4. Add 3 more cups of water and all ingredients except *pakories*. Chill in the fridge.
5. To serve, pour in glasses filled with a little ice and sprinkle some *pakories* on top.

Punjabi Kanji

Red purple drink - The wine of Punjab

Serves 12

½ kg fresh black carrots - peeled and cut into thin fingers, 3 fully heaped tsp of *rai* powder
3 heaped tsp of salt, 2 pinches red chilli powder, ½ tsp black salt (*kala namak*)

1. Boil about 2 litres (8 cups, almost a *patila* full) water. When the water boils, remove pan from fire.
2. Add the carrots. Let them be in hot water for 4-5 minutes.
3. Add 2 more litres (8 more cups) of water and keep aside to cool. Let the water cool completely.
4. Add *rai* powder, salt, red chilli powder and black salt. Mix well.
5. Transfer to an earthern or ceramic jar & keep in the sun for 2-3 days. Stir it every day.
6. After 2-3 days when it turns sour, it can be kept in the refrigerator and used as required. It is served chilled along with a few pieces of carrots.

NOTE:

Rai powder should be added only after the water turns cold.

If black carrots are not available, ordinary carrots and 1 beetroot may be used.

Soups/Shorbas

soups shorbas

Indian soups may sound a little weird but the peppery Mulligatawny Soup originated in the South of India. Shorbas are thin soups which are tempered with Indian spices.

Nimbu Dhania ka Shorba

Serves 4

CLEAR STOCK
rind of 1 lemon, ¼ cup chopped coriander, 2 cloves (*laung*), 1 bay leaf (*tej patta*)
1" piece of ginger - sliced without peeling

OTHER INGREDIENTS
½ cup chopped coriander leaves
1 tbsp oil, 1 tsp cumin seed (*jeera*), 1 tbsp gram flour (*besan*)
2 tbsp roasted peanuts (*moongphali*)- ground to a paste with a little water
½ cup grated carrots, 1-2 cabbage leaves - cut into 1" cubes
1 tsp salt, ½ tsp pepper, or to taste, lemon juice to taste

1. Wash and grate 1 lemon with the peel gently on the grater to get lemon rind. Do not apply pressure and see that the white pith beneath the lemon peel is not grated along with the yellow rind. The white pith is bitter!

2. For stock, mix all ingredients given under stock with 4 cups of water. Bring to a boil. Keep on low flame for 10 minutes. Remove from fire. Strain and keep aside.

3. Heat 1 tbsp oil, add 1 tsp cumin seed. Wait till it turns golden. Reduce heat add 1 tbsp gram flour and stir for ½-1 minute on low heat till it turns golden.

4. Add peanut paste and stir. Add grated carrot and cabbage, stir for ½ a minute.

5. Add the prepared stock. Bring to a boil. Add salt, pepper and lemon juice to taste. Simmer for 2 minutes. Serve in soup bowls, garnished with chopped coriander.

Green Pea Soup

Serves 4

1 cup shelled peas, 1 tbsp butter
3 flakes garlic - crushed, 1 onion - chopped
½ cup milk, salt and pepper to taste
a pinch sugar, ¼ cup grated paneer

1. Heat butter in a pressure cooker. Add garlic & onions. Cook till onions turn transparent.

2. Add peas. Saute for 2-3 minutes on low flame.

3. Add 4 cups of water. Give 3-4 whistles. Remove from fire. After it cools down, blend in a mixer to get a smooth puree. Strain the soup.

4. Add milk. Heat the soup on low heat. Add salt-pepper to taste. Boil for 2 minutes.

5. To serve, boil soup, keeping flame low. Add the grated paneer. Mix, serve hot.

Roasted Tomato Shorba

A thin tomato soup with the authentic Indian flavour.

Serves 8

1 kg (12 big) red tomatoes - washed well
400 ml (2½ cups) water, 2 tsp gram flour (*besan*)
1 cup desiccated coconut (*nariyal ka burada*) or freshly grated coconut
1 tbsp oil, 1 tsp cumin seeds (*jeera*), 10-12 curry leaves, 2-3 green chillies - slit lengthways
1 tsp sugar, or to taste, salt to taste, 1 tsp lemon juice - to taste

GARNISHING
1 tbsp finely chopped fresh coriander leaves, 2-3 tbsp boiled rice - optional

1. Roast whole tomatoes on a naked flame like you do for baingan ka bharta. If tomatoes are small, pierce on a fork and put it on the flame. Peel the skin, and if any black skin remains, let it be. Blend the roasted tomatoes in a mixer to a juice.

2. Strain the tomato juice. Mash the tomatoes in the strainer nicely with a *karchi* to extract all the juice. Keep aside.

3. Grate 1 cup of fresh coconut. Blend it with it's own water in a mixer. If fresh coconut is not available, blend 1 cup desiccated coconut with 2 cups hot water in a mixer.

4. Strain coconut puree to extract milk. Put the unstrained coconut again in the blender with more hot water and churn again. Strain again. Repeat with more water if desired to get 4½ cups coconut milk in all.

5. Add 2 tsp gram flour to the coconut milk and blend well in the mixer. Keep aside.

6. Heat the oil in a pan and add the cumin seeds. After it splutters, add curry leaves, green chillies, tomato juice, coconut milk and sugar.

7. Add salt to taste and cook for 4-5 minutes. Add lemon juice to taste. Garnish with coriander leaves and a few grains of boiled rice. Serve hot.

Spinach Soup

Serves 4-5

3 cups chopped spinach (*paalak*)
1 bay leaf (*tej patta*)
¼" piece ginger - chopped, 1-2 flakes garlic
1 cup milk
salt and pepper to taste

GARNISHING

½ cup roughly mashed paneer
1 tsp lemon juice

1. Boil chopped spinach with a bay leaf, garlic, ginger and 3 cups water. Cover and simmer for 7-8 minutes. Remove from fire. Cool. Puree in a blender.

2. Strain puree. Add salt and pepper to taste. Boil the spinach puree for 2-3 minutes.

3. Reduce heat. Add milk, stirring continuously. Boil again on low heat. Keep aside.

4. To serve, boil soup on low heat. Remove from fire. Add lemon juice, stirring continuously. Garnish with crumbled paneer and serve.

Rasam

A simple South Indian soup with a distinctive flavour.

Serves 4

4 large tomatoes - whole
¼ tsp turmeric (*haldi*) powder, ¼ tsp asafoetida (*hing*) powder, 1½ tsp salt
a tiny piece jaggery (*gur*), coriander leaves for garnishing

RASAM POWDER
5 whole, dry red chillies, 3 tsp coriander seeds, ½ tsp cumin seeds (*jeera*)
¼ tsp mustard (*sarson*) powder, few curry leaves, 1 tsp oil

1. Boil the whole tomatoes on low flame with 1 cup of water for 10 minutes, till they turn soft. Remove from fire and cool.

2. Add 2 cups of water. Mash lightly. Do not put in a blender. Strain the tomato puree. Keep aside.

3. Fry all the ingredients of the rasam powder on very low flame, for 3-4 minutes till the smell of the masalas comes. Remove from fire and powder it finely in a spice grinder.

4. To the tomato puree, add salt, gur and turmeric powder. Boil.

5. Add rasam powder & asafoetida. Cook for 1-2 minutes. Remove from fire. Garnish with coriander leaves.

Mulligatawny Soup

A lentil soup, pepped up with black pepper!

Serves 4-5

¼ cup pink dal (*dhuli masoor dal*) - soaked for atleast 1 hour, or more, 2 onions - chopped
2 carrots - chopped, 1 small apple - peeled and chopped, 1½ tbsp butter
2 vegetable seasoning cubes (maggi) mixed with 5 cups water, 1½ tbsp curry powder
1½ tsp salt, ¾ tsp freshly ground pepper, ¼ cup cooked rice, 1½ tbsp lemon juice, or to taste

GARNISH
1-2 tbsp finely chopped coriander

1. Strain water from the dal. Keep aside.

2. Heat butter. Add onion, carrots and apple. Stir for 3-4 minutes till very light brown.

3. Add curry powder and stir for ½ minute only.

4. Add dal and water mixed with seasoning cubes. Boil. Cover and simmer for 20 minutes or till dal turns soft.

5. Remove from fire. Strain. Spread out the solid part in the strainer in a plate to cool. After it cools, grind to a puree.

6. Add the strained liquid to the puree and mix well.

7. Strain the soup through a soup sieve.

8. Put soup back on fire. Add salt and pepper. Add rice. Cook for 2 minutes.

9. Add lemon juice and remove from fire. Serve hot in soup bowls, garnished with some chopped coriander.

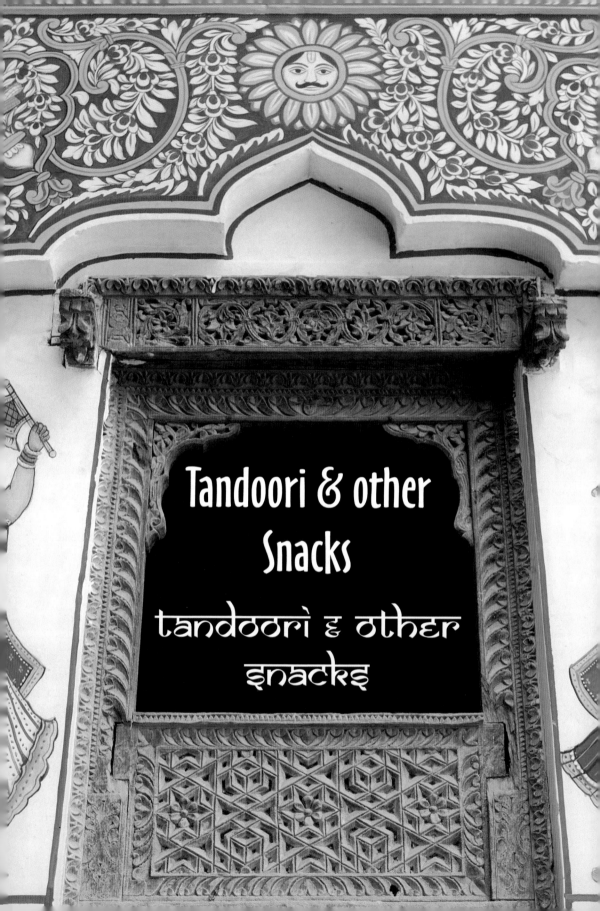

Tandoori & other Snacks

Tips for Snacks...

- The most delicious snack in the world can fail to tempt if it is presented in an unbecoming manner! A greasy or too oily snack is no more appetizing, so make it a habit to remove the fried snack from oil on a tissue or a paper napkin to absorb the excess oil.

- A few crisp leaves of lettuce or a sprig of mint or coriander placed at the edge of the serving platter makes the snack irresistible! Make the green leaves crisp by putting them in a bowl of cold water and keeping them in the fridge for 3-4 hours or even overnight. Some cucumber slices or tomato wedges placed along with the greens, beautify it further.

- For getting a crisp coating on cutlets or rolls, dip prepared snack in a thin batter of *maida* and water and then roll in bread crumbs. Fry till well browned.

- A teaspoon of sesame seeds (*til*) or (poppy seeds) *khus-khus* or carom seeds (*ajwain*), added to coating mixture or bread crumbs makes the snack interesting.

- In the absence of bread crumbs, a mixture of ¼ cup *maida* and ½ cup *suji* may be used to get a crisp coating.

- If your cutlets fall apart, quickly tear 1-2 slices of bread and grind in a mixer to get fresh bread crumbs. Add it to the cutlet mixture for binding.

- To make crisp potato chips, soak them in cold water for 1 hour. Drain. Wipe dry and sprinkle some plain flour (*maida*) on them before frying.

- Never start frying in smoking hot oil as it will turn the snack black. Never fry in cold oil also as the snack may fall apart or it may soak a lot of oil.

- For deep frying any snack, add small quantities to the oil at one time. This maintains the oil's temperature. If too many pieces are added together, the oil turns cold and a lot of oil is then absorbed by the snack.

- After deep frying, let the oil cool down. Add a little quantity of fresh oil to the used oil before reusing. This prevents the oil from discolouring.

Tips for perfect Tandoori Cooking (Barbecuing)...

- Never over grill/cook paneer. It turns hard.

- Marinate vegetable or paneer well in advance, but it should be put in a preheated oven just about 20-30 minutes before serving time, so that it can be served straight from the oven.

- Reheating the paneer can sometimes make it hard. If reheating becomes necessary, brush the *tikka* nicely with some melted butter before putting it in the oven. Also cover it with some foil so that the direct heat does not affect it and make it hard.

- Tandoori food should be barbecued on the grill rack or wire rack (*jaali*) of the oven and not on the oven tray. When the food is put on the tray, the liquid that drips keeps collecting around the food. This does not let the food get crisp on the outside. When it is on the wire rack, the liquid drips down.

- Place a tray beneath the wire rack on which the *tikkas* or any tandoori food is placed. Cover tray with aluminium foil, to collect the drippings of the *tikkas* etc.

- Always grease/brush the wire rack or grill nicely with oil to avoid the kebabs from sticking to grill. If not properly greased, when you pick up done food, marinade comes off as it sticks to grill.

- Cut pieces of vegetable according to the space in between the wires of grill. If the distance between the wires of the rack is too wide, & there is a chance of your piece slipping, then cover the wire rack with a greased aluminium foil.

- Grilling or roasting should be done on constant moderate heat & not on very high heat. High heat makes paneer, shrink & turn hard.

- The size of the *tikkas* should not be too small, because after getting cooked they shrink. A very small piece after getting cooked can turn hard after some time.

- While threading vegetable, skewers should be pushed gently, they should be woven through the *tikka*. This way there are less chances of vegetable slipping down.

- To keep tandoori food soft and succulent, baste food with some melted butter/oil or sometimes with the left over marinade. To baste, just pour the oil/melted butter on food that is being barbecued when it is a little more than ½ done.

Matar Makhana Tikri

Delicious crunchy green tikkis. Very appetizing to look at!

Makes 8

1 cup boiled or frozen shelled peas (*matar*)
1 cup puffed lotus seeds (*makhanas*), 2-3 tbsp cashewnuts (*kaju*)
1 tbsp oil, 2 green chillies - chopped, ¾ tsp salt or to taste, ½ tsp pepper
¼ tsp garam masala, seeds of 4-5 green cardamoms (*chhoti elaichi*)

1. Heat 1 tbsp oil in kadhai. Add *makhanas* and saute for 3-4 minutes.

2. Add cashewnuts and saute till *kaju* starts changing colour. Remove puffed lotus seeds and cashewnuts from the kadhai.

3. In the same kadhai (without any oil leftover), add peas and saute for 2 minutes. Remove peas from kadhai.

4. Grind peas with green chillies to a fine paste in a mixer.

5. Grind fried puffed lotus seeds and cashewnuts together to a rough powder in a mixer.

6. Mix puffed lotus seeds & pea paste. Add salt, pepper, garam masala & green cardamoms.

7. Makes small balls and flatten them to get small round tikkis.

8. Shallow fry on *tawa* or pan in 1-2 tbsp oil till brown and crisp. Serve hot.

Chatpati Dal Papdi

Serves 4

¼ cup split green gram without skin (*moong dhuli dal*)
¼ cup gram dal (*channe ki dal*), ½ cup grated coconut
1 tbsp oil, 2 green chillies - chopped, 1 tsp finely chopped ginger - chopped
2 tbsp chopped coriander, 1 cup grated cucumber (*kheera*) - squeeze lightly
½ tsp black salt, 1 tbsp lemon, ½ tsp chat masala
2 tbsp imli chutney, ready made or home made

TO SERVE
15-20 papdis

1. Soak both dals together in hot water for 1 hour till soft.
2. Heat 1 tbsp oil. Add dals and saute on low heat for 3-4 minutes. Add ½ tsp salt and mix well for a minute. Remove from pan.
3. Mix dals, coconut, chopped green chillies, ginger, coriander, black salt, chat masala and lemon juice in a serving bowl.
4. At serving time, add imli chutney and mix well. Add cucumber and toss lightly. Serve at room temperature topped on papdis.

Stuffed Khandvi

Serves 6-8

½ cup gram flour (*besan*)
½ cup yogurt (*dahi*) (not too sour) mixed with 1 cup water to get 1½ cups butter milk (*lassi*)
¼ tsp turmeric (*haldi*) powder, ¼ tsp cumin seeds (*jeera*) powdered
½ tsp coriander (*dhania*) powder
a pinch of asafoetida (*hing*), 1 tsp salt

PASTE
½" piece ginger, 1-2 green chillies

FILLING
1 tbsp oil, ½ tsp mustard seeds (*rai*)
2 tbsp grated fresh coconut, 1 tbsp grated carrot
1 tsp raisins (*kishmish*) - chopped, 1 tbsp chopped fresh coriander, 2 pinches salt

CHOWNK (TEMPERING)
½ tsp mustard seeds (*rai*), 2-3 green chillies - cut into thin long pieces
some chopped coriander and 1 tbsp grated fresh coconut - for garnish

1. Mix gram flour with 1½ cups buttermilk till smooth. Leaving the chownk and filling ingredients, mix all other ingredients as well as the ginger-chilli paste.

2. Spread a cling film (plastic sheet) on the backside of a big tray.

3. Keep the mixture on low heat in a non stick pan. Cook this mixture for about 25 minutes, stirring, till the mixture becomes very thick and translucent. Drop 1 tsp mixture on the tray and spread. Let it cool for a while and check if it comes out easily. If it does, remove from fire, otherwise cook for another 5 minutes. Remove from fire.

4. While the mixture is still hot, quickly spread some mixture as thinly and evenly as possible on the cling film. Level it with a knife.

5. For the filling, heat oil. Add mustard seeds. After it crackles, add coconut, carrot, kishmish and chopped coriander. Add salt. Mix. Remove from fire.

6. After the mixture cools, cut breadth wise into 2" wide strips. Neaten the 4 border lines with a knife. Put 1 tsp filling at one end. Roll each strip, loosening with a knife initially, to get small cylinders.

7. For chownk, heat 1½ tbsp oil in a pan, add mustard seeds, wait for a minute. Add green chillies. Remove from fire and pour the oil on the khandvis arranged in the plate. Garnish with coconut and coriander.

Matar Kachori

Makes 10

2 cups shelled peas, 2 tbsp gram flour (*besan*)
2 tsp finely chopped ginger, 3-4 green chillies - finely chopped
2 tbsp oil, 1 tsp cumin seeds (*jeera*)
1 tbsp coriander seeds (*sabut dhania*) - split with rolling pin (*belan*)
a pinch of asafoetida (*hing*), ½ tsp crushed black pepper
1 tsp sugar, 1 tsp salt, ¾ tsp garam masala
¼ tsp red chilli powder, ½ tsp dry mango powder (*amchoor*)
oil for deep frying

DOUGH
2 cups plain flour (*maida*), 6 tbsp melted ghee, ¼ tsp baking soda (*mitha soda*)
½ tsp salt, ¼-½ cup water to knead, approx.

1. Mix all ingredients of the dough. Adding enough water, knead into a firm, smooth ball. Knead well for 5-7 minutes. Cover and keep aside.

2. Boil 6-7 cups water with a tsp of sugar. Add the peas and boil for about 8-10 minutes till very soft, strain peas. Transfer to a flat plate. Coarsely crush or mash peas with a potato masher.

3. Heat 2 tbsp oil. Add crushed coriander seeds, cumin and asafoetida. When cumin turns golden, add gram flour and stir for 2 minutes on low heat. Add peas, green chillies and ginger. Saute for 2-3 minutes. Add all the other ingredients.

4. For the kachori, roll a lemon sized ball of the dough into a 2" circle. Make a cup of the disc and stuff 1 heaped tbsp filling in it. Cover filling with the dough. Seal the ends by pinching the top. Flatten with the palms into a 2½" diameter circle. Roll lightly with a rolling pin to make it uniform.

5. Heat oil for frying. Remove oil from fire. Wait for 1-2 minutes. Put 4-5 kachories together in oil. Return to heat & now fry on low heat for about 7-8 minutes till they turn golden brown & the top covering gets cooked properly. Serve hot.

Lachhedar Paneer Crisps

An extremely crisp snack coated with thin vermicelli (long, thin, seviyaan).

Makes 12-14

2½ cups grated paneer (250 gms)
3 slices bread - churned in a mixer to get fresh bread crumbs, ½ cup chopped coriander
¾ tsp chaat masala, ½ tsp roasted cumin (*bhuna jeera*), ¾ tsp salt, ½ tsp pepper

FILLING

¼ cup channa dal - soaked for 2 hours , 1 onion - chopped finely
1 tsp ginger - chopped finely, 1 tbsp cashewnuts (*kaju*) - chopped
2 tbsp raisins (*kishmish*) - chopped, 1 tbsp oil, ¼ tsp turmeric (*haldi*), ½ tsp salt
¼ tsp chilli powder, ¼ tsp dry mango powder (*amchoor*), ½ tsp garam masala

TO COAT

½ cup very thin, long seviyaan- roughly broken into small pieces by hand

1. Strain dal and roughly grind in a mixer to a coarse thick paste. Do not grind too much
2. Heat oil. Add onion, ginger, cashewnuts and raisins. Cook till onions turn light golden.
3. Add ground dal, turmeric, salt, red chilli powder, dry mango powder and garam masala. Stir for 1-2 minutes. Remove from fire and keep aside.
4. Mix paneer, coriander, chaat masala, fresh bread crumbs, roasted cumin, salt & pepper.
5. With a ball of the paneer mixture, make a 2" long oval roll. Flatten it to get a slight depression in the centre. Place 1 tsp of the filling in it along the length. Pick up the sides to cover the filling, such that the filling is completely covered on all sides with the paneer mixture. Shape to give a neat roll with slightly flattened ends.
6. Break seviyaan into 1-1½" small pieces. Spread on a plate. Take 1 cup of water separately in a shallow flat bowl (*katori*). Dip the roll in the water for a second and then immediately roll it over the seviyaan. All the sides should be completely covered with seviyaan.
7. Keep aside to set for 15 minutes. Deep fry 2-3 pieces at a time. Serve with poodina chutney.

Reshmi Paneer Tikka

Tikkas are finished with cream to give them a silky soft taste.

Serves 4-5

250 gms paneer - cut into 1½" cubes (8 pieces)
3 tbsp gram flour (*besan*), 2 tbsp yogurt (*dahi*), 1 tsp salt, ¼ tsp red chilli powder
½ tsp garam masala, a few drops orange red colour, 1 tbsp lemon juice, 2 tbsp oil

GRIND TOGETHER TO A PASTE
3-4 flakes garlic, 1½" piece ginger, 1 tsp cumin seeds (*jeera*)
seeds of 2 cardamoms (*chhoti elaichi*), 2-3 green chillies, 2 tbsp chopped coriander

OTHER INGREDIENTS
4-5 tbsp thick cream, 2 capsicums - cut into 1" pieces
2 onions - cut into 1" pieces, some chaat masala - to sprinkle

1. Mix gram flour, plain flour, yogurt, salt, chilli powder, garam masala, lemon juice, oil & grounded ginger garlic paste. Add enough orange colour to the paste to get a nice colour.

2. Cut paneer into 1½" cubes. Put the paste in a big bowl and add the paneer pieces and mix well so as to coat the paste nicely on all the pieces.

3. At serving time, rub oil generously over the grill of the oven or wire rack of a gas tandoor. Place paneer on the greased wire rack or grill of the oven. Add the onion and capsicum pieces to the little left over marinade and mix well. Keep aside till serving time.

4. Preheat grill for 10 minutes or a gas tandoor on moderate flame. Grill paneer and vegetable for 10 minutes. Spoon some oil on paneer pieces in the oven or tandoor. Grill further for 4-5 minutes.

5. Heat cream in a clean kadhai on very low flame, to make it just warm. Do not let it turn into *ghee* by keeping on the fire for a longer time.

6. Add the grilled paneer and vegetable pieces (onion and capsicum). Toss gently for 2-3 minutes. Serve sprinkled with some chaat masala.

Vegetarian Seekhs

Makes 15

1 cup *saboot masoor ki dal* - soaked for 2 hours in some water
1" piece ginger, 8-10 flakes garlic, 1 green chilli - chopped, 1 tsp cumin seeds (*jeera*)
2 cloves (*laung*) and seeds of 2 green cardamoms (*chhoti elaichi*) - powdered
3 tbsp cornflour, 2 tbsp thick yogurt (*dahi*), 1¼ tsp salt or to taste, 1 tsp garam masala
1 tsp red chilli powder, ¼ tsp dry mango powder (*amchoor*)
½ piece of a bread churned in a mixer to get fresh bread crumbs, 2½ tsp lemon juice
3-4 tbsp oil, 3 tbsp capsicum - chopped, 3 tbsp onion - chopped
2 tbsp tomato (without pulp) - finely chopped

1. Soak *saboot masoor dal* for 2 hours. Strain.

2. Grind dal, ginger, garlic, green chilli and cumin seeds to a thick smooth paste using the minimum amount of water. Keep dal paste aside.

3. Heat 3 tbsp oil in a heavy bottomed kadhai. Add *dal*. Stir-fry for 4-5 minutes on low flame till dal is dry and does not stick to the bottom of the kadhai. Remove.

4. Mix powdered cardamoms, cloves, cornflour, yogurt, salt, garam masala, red chilli powder, dry mango powder and bread crumbs with the dal. Add lemon juice, 2 tbsp of chopped capsicum, 2 tbsp of chopped onion, 1 tbsp of chopped tomato. Reserve the rest. Mix well. Make balls out of the mixture. Keep aside.

5. Take a ball of dal paste and make a 2" long kebab.

6. Take a pencil or a skewer and push it from corner of the kebab to the other without puncturing at any point.

7. Stick remaining chopped onion, capsicum and tomatoes (without pulp) on kebab by pressing vegetables with the palm on to the kebab.

8. Gently pull out the skewer or the pencil.

9. Shallow fry seekh in medium hot oil in a pan to a light brown colour. Serve.

Vegetable Chaat Nuggets

Delicious and soft nuggets with a crisp covering, similar in taste to the pao bhaji mixture.

Serves 4

1 cup chopped cabbage, 1 cup chopped cauliflower (tiny florets), ½ cup shelled peas (*matar*)
2 potatoes - boiled and grated, ½ cup very finely chopped carrots
3 tbsp oil, ½" piece ginger and 3-4 flakes of garlic - crushed or 1 tsp ginger-garlic paste
2½ tsp pao-bhaji masala, 2 bread slices - churned in a mixer to get fresh crumbs
¾ tsp salt, or to taste, ½ tsp sugar, 1 tsp chaat masala, 1 tbsp lemon juice

COATING
½ cup semolina (*suji*), ¼ cup plain flour (*maida*), ½ cup cornflakes - (crush with fingers)
½ tsp salt, ½ tsp pepper

1. Pressure cook cabbage, cauliflower and peas with ½ cup water to give 2 whistles. Reduce heat and keep on low heat for 3-4 minutes. Remove from fire and let the pressure drop. Mash the vegetables. If there is any extra water present, dry it on fire.

2. Heat oil. Add ginger-garlic paste. Stir. Add pao-bhaji masala. Stir for a minute.

3. Add pressure cooked and mashed vegetables. Saute for 2-3 minutes.

4. Add grated potatoes and cook, stirring for 3-4 minutes.

5. Add chopped carrots. Add salt, sugar, chaat masala and lemon juice. Mix well for 2-3 minutes. Remove from fire and let the mixture cool down.

6. Add bread and mix well. Check salt. Shape into tikkis. Flatten to get oval, flat tikkis.

7. For the coating, mix semolina, plain flour, crushed cornflakes, salt and pepper and spread on a plate. Roll tikkis over semolina mixture to coat well. Keep in fridge for 2 hours.

8. At serving time, deep fry 1-2 pieces at a time in medium hot oil till crisp. Remove on paper napkins. Sprinkle some chaat masala and serve hot.

Tandoori Bharwaan Aloo

Serves 6

3 big (longish) potatoes
some chaat masala to sprinkle

FILLING

3 almonds - crushed with a rolling pin (*belan*) or chopped finely
4 tbsp grated paneer (50 gms), 1 tbsp mint (*poodina*) leaves - chopped
1 green chilli - deseeded and chopped, ¼ tsp garam masala, ¼ tsp red chilli powder
¼ tsp salt, a pinch dry mango powder (*amchoor*)

COVERING

½ cup thick yogurt (*dahi*) - hang in a muslin cloth for 30 minutes, 1 tbsp ginger paste
¼ tsp red chilli powder, ¾ tsp salt, ¼ tsp orange tandoori colour or turmeric (*haldi*)

CRUSH TOGETHER TO A ROUGH POWDER

1 tsp black cumin (*shah jeera*), seeds of 2 brown cardamom (*moti elaichi*)
2-3 blades of mace (*javitri*), 6-8 peppercorns (*saboot kali mirch*)

1. Hang yogurt in a muslin cloth for 30 minutes.

2. Boil potatoes in salted water till just tender. When they are no longer hot, peel skin.

3. Mix all the ingredients of the filling together. Mix gently.

4. Grind or crush black cumin, seeds of brown cardamom, 2-3 blades of mace and peppercorns, to a coarse powder.

5. To paneer mixture, add ¼-½ teaspoon of the above freshly ground spice powder also. Keep the leftover powder aside.

6. Mix hung yogurt, ginger paste, red chilli powder, salt, left over freshly ground spice powder. Add turmeric or orange colour.

7. Run the tip of a fork on the surface of the potatoes, making the surface rough. (The rough surface holds the masalas well).

8. Cut each potato into 2 halves, vertically. Scoop out, just a little, to get a small cavity in each potato with the back of a teaspoon. Stuff with paneer filling.

9. With a spoon apply the yogurt mixture on the outside (backside) of the potatoes and on the rim also (not on the filling).

10. Cook potatoes in a gas tandoor or a preheated oven at 210°C/410°F for 15 minutes on a greased wire rack till they get slightly dry.

11. Spoon some oil or melted butter on them (baste) and then cook further for 10 minutes till the coating turns absolutely dry. Sprinkle some chaat masala, serve.

Bhutte Ke Seekh

Corn is very popular in India. Here corn makes a crunchy kebab.

Makes 7-8 pieces

4 tender, large fresh *bhuttas* - grated (1 cup) or 1 cup tinned corn (see note)
2 potatoes - boiled and grated
1 onion - chopped
2 green chillies - chopped finely
3 tbsp chopped fresh coriander
½ tbsp chopped mint (*poodina*)
½ tsp garam masala powder
1 tbsp melted butter
½ tsp pepper powder, 1 tsp salt or to taste
3 tbsp gram flour (*besan*) - roasted on a tawa for 1 minute till fragrant
juice of 1 lemon
3 tbsp melted butter for basting (pouring on the seekhs)

1. Mix the boiled, grated potatoes and the grated corn. Mix well.

2. Add onion, green chillies, coriander, mint, garam masala, 1 tbsp melted butter, pepper and salt. Check seasonings.

3. Add roasted gramflour and lemon juice.

4. Oil and wipe the skewers. Heat an oven to 180°C or a gas tandoor on moderate flame for 15 minutes.

5. Press mixture into sausage-shaped kebabs on the skewers, making a long kebab of the corn paste over the skewer. Cook for about 10 minutes in a hot tandoor or grill. Pour some melted butter on the kebabs to baste them when they get half done. Turn side and grill for 8-10 minutes or till golden brown.

NOTE:

If using tinned corn, instead of fresh corn then blend ½ of the tinned corn in a mixer and keep ½ whole kernels. Mix corn with potatoes, and proceed further in the same way.

If you wish you could even shallow fry the seekhs in a pan on medium heat in 3 tbsp oil.

Oothappam

Makes 6-8

2 cups sela or ushna chaawal (parboiled rice)
½ cup split black gram dal (*dhuli urad dal*)
10 cashewnuts (*kaju*) - split into halves, 2 onions - chopped very finely
2 firm tomatoes - finely chopped, 2-3 green chillies - finely chopped
few curry leaves or coriander - chopped, 1½ tsp salt or to taste

1. Soak rice for 6-7 hours. Soak dal separately for 6 hours. Grind the rice finely.

2. Grind dal very finely to a smooth paste.

3. Mix dal and rice together and add salt. Keep aside in a warm place for 10-12 hours, to get fermented. Add salt to taste. Keep batter aside.

4. Mix onions, tomatoes, chillies, curry patta and salt together in a bowl. Keep aside.

5. Heat a nonstick *tawa*. Put 1 tsp of oil on it. Wipe clean with cloth. Mix batter well, pour 1 *karchhi* (3 tbsp) of batter on it. Spread batter a little, making it slightly thick.

6. Cook for 2-3 minutes till it gets a little cooked from the top. Sprinkle some onion-tomato mixture on the oothappam.

7. Put a few cashewnuts halves. Press the topping with a potato masher or the back of a *karchhi*.

8. Sprinkle 1-2 tsp of oil upon it and also on the sides.

9. Then turn the side carefully, making sure that the underside is cooked before you turn.

10. Remove from *tawa* after the other side also gets cooked and the onions turn light brown.

Tandoori Chaat

Serves 4

2 capsicums - deseed and cut into 1½" pieces (preferably 1 green and 1 red capsicum)
200 gms paneer - cut into 1" cubes (8 pieces), 2 small onions - each cut into 4 pieces
4 fresh pineapple slices - each cut into 4 pieces (see note)
2 tomatoes - each cut into 4 pieces and pulp removed
1 tsp garam masala, 2 tbsp lemon juice, 1 tbsp tandoori masala or barbecue masala
2 tbsp oil, 1 tsp salt, or to taste, 1½ tsp chaat masala

1. Cut paneer into 1" square pieces and capsicum into 1½" pieces.

2. Cut each onion and tomato into 4 pieces. Mix all the vegetables, pineapple and paneer in a bowl.

3. Sprinkle all the ingredients on them. Mix well.

4. Grease the grill or wire rack of the oven or tandoor. Preheat the grill for 10 minutes. Place the paneer, pineapple and onions only on the grill rack. Grill for about 15 minutes, till the edges start to change colour.

5. After the paneer is almost done, put the capsicum and tomatoes also on the wire rack with the paneer etc. Grill for 10 minutes.

6. Remove from the oven straight to the serving plate. Sprinkle some chaat masala and lemon juice, if you like.

NOTE:

If tinned pineapple is being used, grill it in the second batch with capsicum and tomatoes since it is already soft.

Kaju Tomato Idli

Makes 25

2 cups *sela* or *ushna chaawal* (parboiled rice), 1 cup split black gram dal (*dhuli urad dal*)
2 tsp salt or to taste, 1 tsp eno fruit salt, optional

TOPPING

a few cashewnuts (*kaju*) - split into halves, 2-3 small, firm tomatoes - cut into thin slices
a few curry leaves

1. Soak rice for 4-5 hours or overnight. Soak dal for 4-5 hours separately or overnight.

2. Grind the rice coarsely by adding water. It should be like semolina. Do not make it very fine.

3. Grind dal by adding small quantities to the mixer, to a very fine paste. Even after you feel that the dal is ready, grind some more, adding a little water, till the dal turns absolutely smooth and fluffy and a few bubbles can be seen.

4. Mix rice & dal batters together. Add salt. The batter is of thick pouring consistency. Mix well. Keep batter for 8-10 hours or more in a warm place to get fermented properly. It should rise & smell sour. If batter is not fermented properly, add 1 tsp of eno fruit salt. Mix.

5. To make idlis, mix the batter very gently. Wash idli mould. Do not wipe. Grease the mould with oil. Place a tomato slice, a curry patta and a cashewnuts half. Fill with batter.

6. Put 1" water in a big cooker or a big pan with a well fitting lid and place on the gas. Keep it on fire. Place the idli mould inside the cooker and put the lid after removing the whistle. Keep the gas on full flame. After water boils, keep on high flame for 2 minutes.

7. Then keep for 14-15 minutes on medium flame. Insert a clean knife to see if the idli is done. If it sticks to the knife, steam for another 1-2 minutes. Switch off the gas and remove the idlis from the pan after 5 minutes. Serve hot with sambhar and chutney.

Moong Shooters

Vegetable sticks, coated with a moong dal batter and fried. The moong dal coating imparts a special flavour to these sticks.

Serves 4

2 potatoes - boiled and cut into 1" square pieces
1 capsicum - cut into 1" pieces
1 tomato - cut into 4 pieces lengthwise, pulp removed and cut into 1" pieces
some chaat masala

BATTER

1 cup dhuli moong dal (dehusked *moong* beans) - soaked for 1-2 hours
2 tbsp fresh coriander - chopped very finely
1 green chilli - chopped very finely
¾ tsp salt, ½ tsp red chilli powder or less, as desired
1-2 pinches of tandoori red food colour

1. Soak dal for 1-2 hours

2. Cut potatoes into 1" squares.

3. Cut capsicum and tomato into 1" pieces.

4. Strain the soaked dal. Grind in a mixer without water to a smooth thick paste. Put in a bowl. Beat well with hands to make it light.

5. Add coriander, green chilli, salt and red chilli powder to the dal paste. Add enough tandoori colour to get a bright orange colour. Keep aside.

6. Sprinkle chaat masala nicely on paneer, capsicum and tomato pieces. Mix lightly.

7. Thread a capsicum (wrong side facing you), then a potato and then a tomato piece (right side facing you) on each tooth pick. Keep aside till serving time.

8. To serve, heat oil for deep frying. Dip the potato sticks in the prepared dal batter. Coat well with the fingers, sticking the batter nicely.

9. Deep fry till golden. Serve sprinkled with some chaat masala.

NOTE:
You can use paneer instead of boiled potatoes.

Masala Dosa

Serves 4

BATTER

2 cups sela or *ushna chaawal* (parboiled) rice of ordinary quality
1 cup *permal chaawal* (ordinary quality rice)
¾ cup *dhuli urad dal*, 2 tsp fenugreek seeds (*methi dana*)
2 tsp salt (to taste), oil for making dosas

POTATO MASALA

4 medium (½ kg) potatoes - boiled, ¼ cup peas - boiled (optional)
2 tbsp oil, ¾ tsp mustard seeds (*sarson*), 1 tsp bengal gram dal (*channe ki dal*)
1 dry, red chilli - broken into pieces, few curry leaves
2 green chillies - chopped, ¼" piece of ginger - chopped
2 small onions - chopped, 1 tbsp cashewnuts - broken into bits
¼ tsp turmeric (*haldi*) powder, ¼ tsp red chilli powder, salt to taste

44

1. To prepare the batter, soak both the rice, dal & fenugreek seeds together in a pan for at least 6 hours.

2. Grind together finely to a paste, using some of the water in which it was soaked.

3. Add more water to the paste, if required, to get a paste of medium pouring consistency.

4. Add salt. Mix well.

5. Keep aside for 12 hours or over-night in a warm place, to get fermented. After fermentation, the batter rises a little and smells sour.

6. After the batter is ready, prepare the masala. Boil the potatoes. Peel & mash them roughly.

7. Heat 2 tbsp oil in a kadahi. Reduce flame & add ¾ tsp mustard seeds, 1 tsp channe ki dal and 1 dry red chilli.

8. When dal changes colour, add curry leaves, ginger, green chilli stir fry for 2 minutes on low flame.

9. Add onion. Cook till transparent. Add cashewnuts, salt, turmeric & red chilli powder. Fry for 1 minute.

10. Add 1 cup water. Boil & keep covered on low flame for 5-7 minutes or till the dal turns soft.

11. Add the mashed potatoes & peas. Cook for 5 minutes. Mix well. Remove from fire. Keep masala aside.

12. To prepare the dosa, mix the batter nicely with a *karchhi*.

13. Heat a non stick *tawa* on medium flame. Pour a tsp oil on the *tawa*. Sprinkle 2-3 pinches salt. Rub the oil gently with piece of old cloth.

14. Remove the pan from fire & pour 1 heaped *karchhi* of batter. Spread quickly, but lightly.

15. Return to fire. Cook till the dosa get a little cooked.

16. Pour 2 tsp of oil upon the dosa & on the sides.

17. After golden brown spots appear, gently loosen the sides and the bottom.

18. Put 2 tbsp masala in the centre & spread a little. Fold over from both sides. Remove from *tawa*.

19. Place a blob of white butter on the dosa & serve hot with coconut chutney & sambhar.

Kathal Tikka

Serves 6

300 gms of jack fruit (*kathal*), a pinch of turmeric (*haldi*)
2 tbsp oil - to baste (pour on the tikka)

MARINADE

1 cup thick yogurt (*dahi*) - hang in a muslin cloth for 1 hour
1 tbsp tandoori masala, 1 tbsp ginger paste, ¼ tsp red chilli powder, ¾ tsp salt, 1 tbsp oil
a pinch of tandoori colour or turmeric (*haldi*) powder, crush together to a rough powder
½ tsp roasted cumin (*bhuna jeera*), seeds of 2 green cardamom (*chhoti elaichi*)
2-3 blades of mace (*javitri*), 3-4 peppercorns (*saboot kali mirch*)

1. Hang yogurt in a muslin cloth for ½ hour.

2. Rub oil on your hands. Cut the whole big piece of kathal from the middle into two pieces. Remove skin. Cut widthwise from the centre of each piece. This way you get two big strips of kathal. Now further divide each strip into smaller pieces about 1" thickness, carefully to keep the shreds of the piece together. Then further divide into ½" thick pieces.

3. Boil 7-8 cups of water with 2 tsp salt and a pinch of turmeric. Add kathal and boil for 10 minutes till crisp-tender. Keep aside.

4. Grind or crush roasted cumin, seeds of green cardamoms, peppercorns and 2-3 pinches of mace to a rough powder.

5. Mix all the ingredients of the marinade and freshly ground green cardamom-peppercorns powder. Mix in jack fruit. Let it marinate for an hour in the refrigerator.

6. Place the tikkas on a greased wire rack. Roast in a gas tandoor or a preheated oven at 180°C for 15 minutes or till the coating gets slightly dry.

7. Spoon some oil or melted butter on it (baste) and cook further for 10 minutes till coating turns absolutely dry. Sprinkle some chaat masala.

8. Serve hot with poodina chutney.

Curries

CURRIES

Khumb Matar Miloni

Serves 4

1 packet (200 gms) mushrooms *(khumb)*
1 cup peas (shelled) - boiled
2 tbsp oil, 1 tsp ginger-garlic paste
¼ tsp turmeric *(haldi)* powder
1 tbsp dry fenugreek leaves *(kasoori methi)*
1¼ tsp salt or to taste, ½ tsp garam masala
½ tsp degi mirch or red chilli powder

PASTE - 1

2 onions, 2 cloves *(laung)*, 2 seeds green cardamoms *(chhoti elaichi)*, 1 tsp fennel *(saunf)*

PASTE - 2

3 tomatoes - put in boiling water for 3 minutes (blanched), peeled and cut into 4
½ cup yogurt, 2 tbsp cashewnuts *(kaju)*

1. Trim stalks of mushroom and cut each into 4 pieces.

2. Heat 2 tbsp oil add mushrooms and saute for 4-5 minutes. Keep them spaced out while sauteing.

3. Add ginger- garlic paste. Cook for a minute. Remove from fire.

4. Grind all the ingredients of paste - 1 to a smooth paste. Keep aside.

5. Grind all the ingredients of paste - 2 to a smooth paste. Keep aside.

6. For masala, heat 3 tbsp oil. Add paste- 1. Cook till light brown. Add turmeric powder.

7. Add paste- 2. Stir for 8-10 minutes or till dry and oil separates.

8. Add fenugreek leaves and degi mirch or red chilli powder. Mix.

9. Add 2 cups water. Boil. Add salt, garam masala and fried mushrooms and boiled peas. Mix. Remove and serve curry with rice or *chappatis*.

Rajasthani Bharwaan Lauki

Roundels of bottle gourd stuffed with paneer.

Serves 4-6

500 gms bottle gourd (*lauki*) - choose *lauki* of medium thickness

FILLING
200 gms paneer - crumbled (mash roughly)
1 tsp finely chopped ginger, 1 green chilli - finely chopped
2 tbsp chopped green coriander
8-10 cashewnuts (*kaju*) - chopped
8-10 raisins (*kishmish*) - soaked in water
¾ tsp salt or to taste

MASALA
2 tbsp oil or ghee
2 cloves (*laung*), 2 bay leaves (*tej patta*)
2 green cardamoms (*chhoti elaichi*)
1" stick cinnamon (*dalchini*)

TOMATO PASTE (Grind Together)
3 tomatoes
1 green chilli, ½" piece ginger
½ tsp red chilli powder, 1 tsp coriander (*dhania*) powder, ¼ tsp turmeric (*haldi*) powder
¾ tsp salt, ½ tsp cumin seeds (*jeera*), ¼ tsp sugar

1. Peel bottle gourd. Cut vertically into two pieces from the centre to get 2 smaller pieces.
2. Boil in salted water, covered, for about 10 minutes, till done. Remove from water and cool. Scoop seeds from both the pieces of the bottle gourd and make them hollow.
3. Grind all the ingredients given under tomato paste to a smooth paste in a grinder.
4. For filling - mix paneer, ginger, green chilli, coriander, cashewnuts, raisins and salt.
5. Stuff it into the boiled bottle gourd pieces. Keep aside.
6. For masala - heat ghee. Add cloves, cardamoms, cinnamon and bay leaves. Stir for a minute.
7. Add the prepared tomato paste. Stir for 3-4 minutes till thick and oil separates.
8. Add 1½ cups water. Boil. Simmer for 4-5 minutes till oil separates. Keep aside.
9. At serving time, saute whole bottle gourd pieces in a non stick pan in 1 tbsp oil, turning sides carefully to brown from all sides. Remove from pan.
10. Pour half of the hot gravy in a dish. Cut the bottle gourd into ¾" thick round pieces and arrange over the gravy. Pour the remaining hot tomato gravy on top. Heat in a microwave if you like. Serve.

Mewa Seekh in Gravy

Do not get put off by the long list of ingredients, the final product is delicious.
The seekhs are simple to make and the ingredients are easily available!
The gravy can also be used with simply fried paneer, or baby corns or any koftas.

Serves 4

¾ cups grated paneer (75 gms)
a few toothpicks
¼ cup dry bread crumbs, 1 tsp cornflour
¼ tsp garam masala, ¼-½ tsp salt or to taste
¼ tsp red chilli powder, a pinch of dry mango powder (*amchoor*)

DRY ROAST ON A TAWA

1 tsp sunflower seeds (*chironji*) or 1 tsp chopped almonds (*badam*)
1 tsp melon seeds (*magaz*)

PASTE (GRIND TOGETHER)

½" piece ginger, 3-4 flakes garlic, 1 green chilli, 3 tbsp green coriander, 5 cashewnuts (*kaju*)
4 almonds (*badaam*), 3 raisins (*kishmish*), 2- 3 whole pistachio (*pistas*)
¼ tsp nutmeg (*jaiphal*), ¼ tsp mace (*javetri*)

GRAVY

2 onions, ½" piece of ginger and 3-4 flakes of garlic - ground to a paste
1 tsp ginger-garlic paste, 4 tbsp dry fenugreek leaves (*kasoori methi*)
½ cup fresh cream or thin malai
3 tbsp oil, 1 tbsp butter
1 tsp salt, or to taste, ½ tsp red chilli powder
½ tsp garam masala, a pinch of dry mango powder (*amchoor*)
1 cup milk (approx.)

POWDER (GRIND TOGETHER)

½" stick cinnamon (*dalchini*), seeds of 2-3 green cardamom (*chhoti elaichi*)
3-4 cloves (*laung*), 4-5 peppercorns (*saboot kali mirch*), 2 tbsp cashewnuts (*kaju*)

1. Roast melon seeds and sunflower seeds/almonds on a *tawa* on low heat. Cool.

2. Grind all the ingredients given under paste in a mixer to a paste.

3. Mix together - ¼ cup bread crumbs, cornflour, garam masala, salt, red chilli powder, dry mango powder, grated paneer, roasted sunflower seeds/almonds, melon seeds, and the prepared paste. Mix well.

4. Take a lemon sized ball of the mixture. Make a small roll of 1½" length. Flatten it from the sides. Insert a toothpick from one flattened end to the other, going straight out of the roll, without puncturing the roll at any other point. Repeat with the left over mixture. Keep the seekhs covered with a cling wrap in the refrigerator for atleast ½ hour so that they get set properly.

5. Grind all the ingredients given under powder together on a *chakla belan* or in a small spice grinder. Keep aside the powder.

6. For the gravy, heat 3 tbsp oil and 1 tbsp butter. Add onion-garlic paste and cook on low heat till oil separates. Do not let the onions turn brown.

7. Add the freshly ground masala-cashewnuts powder. Cook for a few seconds.

8. Add dry fenugreek leaves and cream, cook on low heat for 2-3 minutes till cream dries up.

9. Add salt, red chilli powder, garam masala and amchoor. Stir for 1 minute.

10. Add 1 cup milk and ½ cup water. Boil for 1 minute on low heat. Remove from fire.

11. Heat oil in a kadhai. Remove seekhs from the fridge. Deep fry the seekhs one at a time alongwith the toothpicks till golden brown. Drain on paper napkins. Keep aside till serving time.

12. At serving time, heat sticks and gravy separately. Pour the hot gravy in a serving dish and arrange the hot sticks over it. If you want, put some gravy in the serving dish, arrange seekhs and again pour the rest of the gravy on top. If you like, you can heat the seekhs in gravy together, in a microwave. Serve hot.

Punjabi Sarson ka Saag

Serves 6

1 bundle (1 kg) mustard greens (*sarson*)
250 gms spinach (*paalak*) or *baathoo*
2 turnips (*shalgam*) - peeled and chopped, optional
3-4 flakes garlic - finely chopped, optional
2" piece ginger - finely chopped
1 green chilli - chopped
¾ tsp salt, or to taste
2 tbsp maize flour (*makki ka atta*)
1½ tsp powdered jaggery (*gur*)

TADKA/TEMPERING
3 tbsp desi ghee
1" piece ginger - finely chopped
2 green chillies - finely chopped
½ tsp red chilli powder

1. Wash and clean mustard leaves. First remove the leaves and then peel the stems, starting from the lower end and chop them finely. (Peel stems the way you string green beans). The addition of stems to the *saag* makes it tastier but it is important to peel the stems from the lower ends. The upper tender portion may just be chopped. Chop the spinach or *baathoo* leaves and mix with sarson.

2. Put chopped greens with ½ cup water in a pan.

3. Chop garlic, ginger and green chilli very finely and add to the *saag*, add turnips if you wish. Add salt and put it on fire and let it start heating.

4. The *saag* will start going down. Cover and let it cook on medium fire for 15-20 minutes. Remove from fire, cool.

5. Grind to a coarse paste. Do not grind too much and make it very smooth.

6. Add maize flour to the saag and cook for 15 minutes on low heat.

7. For *tadka*, heat desi ghee. Reduce heat and add ginger and green chillies. Cook till ginger changes colour. Remove from fire and add red chilli powder. Add ghee to the hot saag and mix lightly. Serve hot.

8. Serve with fresh home-made butter and makki-ki-roti.

NOTE:
Fresh saag should have tender leaves and tender stems (gandal).

Paneer Makhani

Serves 4

250 gms paneer - cut into 1" cubes
5 large (500 gms) tomatoes - each cut into 4 pieces
2 tbsp desi ghee or butter and 2 tbsp oil
4-5 flakes garlic and 1" piece ginger - ground to a paste (1½ tsp ginger-garlic paste)
1 tbsp dry fenugreek leaves (*kasoori methi*), 1 tsp tomato ketchup
½ tsp cumin seeds (*jeera*), 2 tsp coriander (*dhania*) powder, ½ tsp garam masala
1 tsp salt, or to taste, ½ tsp red chilli powder, preferably degi mirch
½ cup water, ½-1 cup milk, approx., ½ cup cream (optional)
3 tbsp cashewnuts (*kaju*)

1. Soak cashewnuts in a little warm water for 10-15 minutes.

2. Drain cashewnuts. Grind in a mixer to a very smooth paste using about 2 tbsp water.

3. Boil tomatoes in ½ cup water. Simmer for 4-5 minutes on low heat till tomatoes turn soft. Remove from fire and cool. Grind the tomatoes along with the water to a smooth puree.

4. Heat oil and ghee or butter in a kadhai. Reduce heat. Add cumin seeds. When it turns golden, add ginger-garlic paste.

5. When paste starts to change colour add the above tomato puree and cook till dry.

6. Add dry fenugreek leaves and tomato ketchup.

7. Add masalas - coriander powder, garam masala, salt and red chilli powder. Mix well for a few seconds. Cook till oil separates.

8. Add cashew paste. Mix well for 2 minutes.

9. Add water. Boil. Simmer on low heat for 4-5 minutes. Reduce heat.

10. Add the paneer cubes. Remove from fire. Keep aside to cool for about 5 minutes.

11. Add enough milk to the cold paneer masala to get a thick curry, mix gently. (Remember to add milk only after the masala is no longer hot, to prevent the milk from curdling. After adding milk, heat curry on low heat.)

12. Heat on low heat, stirring continuously till just about to boil.

13. Add cream, keeping the heat very low and stirring continuously. Remove from fire immediately and transfer to a serving dish. Swirl 1 tbsp cream over the hot paneer in the dish. Serve immediately.

VARIATION:

For dakshini tadka, heat 1 tbsp oil. Add ½ tsp rai. After 30 seconds add 4-5 curry leaves. Stir. Remove from fire. Add a pinch of red chilli powder and pour over the hot paneer makhani in the dish.

Kashmiri Dum Aloo

Paneer stuffed aloos in a delicious subtle Kashmiri gravy. Must give it a try!

Serves 4- 6
6 medium potatoes, oil for frying

FILLING
100 gms paneer (cottage cheese) - grated
1 small onion - finely chopped, 1 green chilli - chopped finely
4- 5 cashewnuts (*kaju*) - chopped, 8-10 raisins (*kishmish*) - chopped
1 tbsp oil, salt to taste

GRAVY
1 bay leaf (*tej patta*), 1 tsp royal cumin (*shah jeera*)
4 tbsp very finely grated *khoya*, 1½ tbsp dry fenugreek leaves (*kasoori methi*)
1½ tsp salt or to taste, ½ tsp garam masala

ONION PASTE
1 onion, 2 cloves (*laung*), ¾" piece of ginger, 4- 5 flakes of garlic
seeds of 2 green cardamoms (*chhoti elaichi*), 2 tbsp fennel seeds (*saunf*)
seeds of 2 black cardamoms (*moti elaichi*), 1" stick cinnamon (*dalchini*)

TOMATO PASTE
4 tomatoes - blanched and pureed in a mixer, ¼ tsp nutmeg (*jaiphal*)
¼ tsp mace (*javitri*) powder, 2½ tbsp cashewnuts (*kaju*)
2 dry, red chillies, 2 tbsp poppy seeds (*khus-khus*)

1. Peel and wash the potatoes. Prick with a fork. Scoop out the inner portion of the potato with a scooper or the back of a potato peeler. Leave a wall of ¼" all around the potato.

2. Keep the potatoes in salted water for 15 minutes. Strain and pat dry.

3. Heat oil and deep fry all potatoes together till they get cooked properly and are golden brown in colour. Take out 1 piece from oil and check to see if cooked. If done, then remove all pieces from the *kadhai* on paper napkins. Keep aside till serving time.

4. For filling, heat 1 tbsp oil, add onion and green chilli. Cook till onion turns light golden.

5. Add cashewnuts and raisins. Cook for 1 minute.

6. Add grated paneer and salt. Cook for a few seconds. Remove from fire and cool.

7. Fill potatoes with prepared filling. Press well. Keep aside.

8. Grind all the ingredients of onion paste to a smooth paste. Keep aside.

9. Grind all the ingredients of tomato paste to a smooth paste. Keep aside.

10. For gravy - heat 3 tbsp oil, add bay leaf and royal cumin, wait for a minute.

11. Add onion paste. Cook for 2- 3 minutes till golden brown.

12. Add tomato paste. Stir for 4-5 minutes or till oil separates.

13. Add *khoya*, dry fenugreek leaves, salt and garam masala. Cook for 2 minutes, stirring. Add ¾ cup of water. Boil. Simmer for 3 minutes. Remove from fire and keep aside till serving time.

14. At serving time, add 1 cup milk and boil on low heat.

15. Add fried potatoes. Keep on fire for 2-3 minutes. Serve hot.

Baghare Baingan

Serves 4

250 gms (8-10 pieces) brinjals (small, round variety)
½ tsp *shakkar* or powdered jaggery (*gur*)
½" piece ginger - chopped, 5-6 flakes garlic - chopped
1 tbsp roasted peanuts - crushed on a *chakla belan*
1 tbsp fresh coriander leaves
3/4 tsp salt, ½ tsp red chilli powder, ¼ tsp garam masala
6-7 tbsp oil
1 big onion - finely grated
½ tsp fennel (*saunf*) seeds - crushed on a *chakla*
1 tsp full tamarind (a small marble sized ball)

ROAST TOGETHER
2 tsp freshly grated or desiccated (powdered) coconut
2 tsp sesame seeds (*til*), 2 tsp coriander seeds (*saboot dhania*)
½ tsp cumin seeds (*jeera*)

1. Slit brinjals to give 2 cross cuts, almost till the end, but keep the end together.

2. Soak a small marble sized ball of tamarind in ¼ cup of warm water for 15 minutes. Strain and rub well to extract pulp. Keep aside.

3. Roast coconut, sesame seeds, cumin and coriander seeds on a tawa on low flame for about 2 minutes, till they just change colour and become fragrant.

4. Grind the roasted ingredients along with gur, ginger, garlic and coriander leaves with 2-3 tbsp water to a paste.

5. Add salt, red chilli powder, garam masala and crushed peanuts. Mix well. Fill this masala into the brinjals.

6. Heat 6-7 tbsp oil in a non stick pan or a large kadhai. Add brinjals, one by one, arranging in the pan or kadhai. Turn side after 2 minutes. Reduce heat and cover and cook on low heat, for about 15 minutes, till they turn soft. Change sides once in between. Feel with a knife if the brinjals have turned soft. Remove from oil and keep aside. Remove all the masala also from the oil.

7. Heat the leftover oil and add crushed saunf. When it changes colour, add onion and cook to a light golden colour. Add ½ tsp of salt and ½ tsp red chilli powder.

8. Add tamarind juice. Mix. Add brinjals, cover and cook for 5 minutes, on low heat, stirring occasionally taking care not to break the brinjals. Serve hot.

Gatte ki Kadhi

Kadhi is a thick liquid made by blending gram flour with yogurt and simmering it gently. Dumplings or vegetables can be added, but here you find the addition of a typical Rajasthani food, gatte, spongy cubes made from a well-spiced gram flour dough.

Serves 4

GATTE
1½ cups gram flour (*besan*), 1 tbsp yogurt (*dahi*)
a pinch of baking soda (*mitha soda*), ¾ tsp carom seeds (*ajwain*)
¾ tsp coriander seeds (*sabut dhania*), 1 tsp anardana
2 tbsp oil
1 green chilli -finely chopped, 1 tbsp green coriander - finely chopped
8-10 mint leaves - finely chopped, 1 tsp salt, or to taste

KADHI
2 cups yogurt, 2 tbsp gram flour (*besan*)
1 tsp cumin seeds (*jeera*), 1 tsp mustard seeds (*rai* or *sarson*)
½ tsp fennel (*saunf*), a pinch of asafoetida (*hing*)
1 tsp turmeric (*haldi*) powder, 2 tsp red chilli powder
1 tsp coriander (*dhania*) powder, salt to taste
2 tbsp oil
2 tbsp green coriander leaves - finely chopped

1. Mix all the ingredients for gatte together and knead a hard dough using about 4-5 tbsp water Shape dough into cylinders with greased hands as the dough is quite sticky.

2. Boil gatte in water for 10-12 minutes till they turn slightly yellowish white.

3. Keep these aside and cut them into 1 inch pieces.

4. For the kadhi, mix yogurt and gram flour together, add turmeric powder and salt and mix well.

5. Heat oil in a kadhai, add asafoetida, cumin seeds and mustard seeds, when they start spluttering add fennel. Wait till it changes colour.

6. Add yogurt-gram flour mixture. Add 4-5 cups of water. Bring to a boil, add red chilli powder and coriander powder and the gatte, cook the kadhi on low heat for 20-25 minutes. Serve with rice/roti.

Avial

A variety of vegetables are served in a yogurt-based white gravy that is thickened with rice powder and grated coconut.

Serves 4

1 raw banana - cut into 1" long strips
1 small carrot - cut into 1" long strips
4 beans - cut into 1" thin long strips
2 small drumsticks - cut into 1" strips
1 small potato - cut into 1" long strips or 100 gms yam - cut into 1" long strips
1 tsp salt, ¼ tsp turmeric (*haldi*) powder
2 tbsp coconut oil
few curry leaves
½ tsp mustard seeds (*sarson*)
2 dry red chillies

PASTE

½ fresh coconut - grated, 1 tsp cumin seeds (*jeera*), 3-4 green chillies
¾ cup yogurt (*dahi*), 2 tsp rice powder

1. Boil 4-5 cups water. Add 1 tsp salt and ¼ tsp turmeric. Add vegetables. Boil for 2 minutes till slightly soft. Drain and keep aside.

2. Grind all ingredients of the paste till smooth.

3. Add 1½ cups water to the paste and keep on low heat, stirring continuously till it boils.

4. Add vegetables and simmer for a minute. Remove the avial from heat.

5. Heat 2 tbsp coconut oil. Add mustard seeds. Reduce heat. Add curry leaves and red chillies. Pour tempering on the avial. Serve hot.

Haryali Bhutte ke Kofte

Corn koftas in green spinach gravy.

Serves 4

4 tender, large fresh bhuttas - grated (1 cup)
2 potatoes - boiled and grated
1 onion - chopped
2 green chillies - chopped finely
3 tbsp chopped fresh coriander
½ tsp garam masala powder
½ tsp pepper powder, 1 tsp salt or to taste
3 tbsp gramflour (*besan*) - roasted on a tawa for 1 minute till fragrant

GRAVY

250 gms spinach (*paalak*) - chopped (2½ cups)
2 onions - ground to a paste
3 tbsp desi ghee or 4 tbsp oil
¼ tsp turmeric (*haldi*) powder, ½ tsp garam masala, ½ tsp salt, or to taste

TOMATO PASTE

1 tomato, 1" piece ginger, 5 flakes garlic, 2 green chillies

1. Mix the boiled, grated potatoes and the grated corn. Mix well. Add onion, green chillies, coriander, garam masala, pepper and salt.

2. Add roasted gramflour. Check seasonings. Make balls.

3. Roll in dry plain flour and deep fry one at a time to a golden colour. Keep koftas aside.

4. Discard stems of paalak leaves. Wash leaves in lots of water to remove grains of sand or soil. Pressure cook with ¼ cup water to give one whistle. Keep on low flame for 5-7 minutes. Remove from fire. Cool. Grind in a mixer.

5. Grind 2 onions to a paste.

6. Grind all ingredients of tomato paste to a smooth paste.

7. Heat ghee and add onion paste. Fry till golden in colour.

8. Add tomato paste and cook on low flame for 2-3 minutes.

9. Add turmeric powder, garam masala and salt. Stir for 1 minute.

10. Add ground paalak and cook for 1 minute.

11. Add 2 cups hot water to get a thin green gravy. Boil. Keep on low flame for 10-15 minutes.

12. At serving time, add koftas. Keep on low flame for 1 minute. Serve hot.

Bharwaan Kofte in Magaz Gravy

Serves 4

KOFTA
100 gms paneer, 1 tbsp cornflour
¼ tsp roasted cumin (*jeera*) powder, ¼ tsp red chilli powder, ¼ tsp salt
2 tbsp plain flour (*maida*) - to coat

FILLING OF KOFTAS
few strands saffron (*kesar*) - soaked in 1 tbsp warm milk
1 onion - very finely chopped, ½" piece ginger - very finely chopped
4-5 cashews (*kaju*) - chopped, 10-12 raisins (*kishmish*)
¼ tsp each of salt, garam masala, red chilli powder

GRAVY
2 onions - ground to a paste
1 cup cream (200 gms)
¾ tsp garam masala, ¾ tsp red chilli powder, ¾ tsp salt or to taste
3 green cardamoms (*chhoti elaichi*) - crushed to a powder

PASTE FOR GRAVY
2 tbsp water melon seeds (*magaz*), 2 tbsp cashewnuts (*kaju*), 4 tbsp yogurt

1. Soak cashews and magaz in water for 10 minutes. Drain and grind to a very fine paste with yogurt. Keep aside for gravy.

2. For filling, heat 2 tsp ghee or oil. Add onion and ginger. Fry till light golden brown.

3. Add cashews, raisins, salt, garam masala and red chilli powder. Remove from fire. Add the soaked kesar with the milk. Mix well. Keep aside.

4. For the koftas, mix paneer, cornflour, cumin powder, red chilli powder and salt.

5. Make 8 marble sized balls. Flatten each ball, put 1 tsp of onion filling in each ball. Form a ball again. Roll each ball in maida.

6. Deep fry 2-3 koftas at a time in medium hot oil till golden. Keep aside.

7. For gravy, heat 3 tbsp oil. Add onion paste. Cook on low flame till it turns transparent and oil separates. Do not let it turn brown by keeping on high flame.

8. Add the prepared cashews - magaz paste. Cook for 2-3 minutes on low flame.

9. Add garam masala, red chilli powder and salt.

10. Add cream and 1 cup water. Boil on low heat for 1 minute.

11. At the time of serving, add powdered cardamom and boil the gray.

12. Add koftas and cook for a minute on low heat. Serve garnished with kesar strands.

NOTE:
If the koftas break on frying, add ½ tbsp more of cornflour to the mixture.

Tilli Pe Subz Bahaar

Masala vegetables arranged on toothpicks and served with a spicy gravy.

Serves 4

1 big potato, 5-6 french beans, 2 carrots, a few toothpicks

FOR DRY MASALA (GRIND TOGETHER)
2 tsp coriander seeds (*saboot dhania*)
1½ tsp cumin seeds (*jeera*), 1 tsp red chilli powder, ½ tsp turmeric (*haldi*) powder
6-7 cloves (*laung*), seeds of 6 brown cardamom (*moti elaichi*)
5-8 peppercorns (*saboot kali mirch*)

GRIND TOGETHER
2 onions - roughly chopped, ½" piece ginger - chopped

OTHER INGREDIENTS
3-4 tbsp oil, a pinch of asafoetida (*hing*), 2 tomatoes - chopped
2 tsp of the above dry masala
½ tsp shredded ginger, water - kept aside of the boiled vegetables
¼ tsp dry mango powder (*amchoor*), ½ tsp garam masala, salt to taste

1. Grind all ingredients of the dry masala together. Keep aside 2 tsp from this ground masala separately for the vegetables.

2. Peel potatoes and cut each into ½" pieces or squares. Deep fry to a golden colour.

3. Cut carrots into ¼" thick rounds. String french beans and cut into ½" long pieces.

4. Boil 2 cups of water with ½ tsp salt. Add beans and carrots. Boil for about 5 minutes or till tender. Strain, reserve the water for the gravy.

5. For the curry, heat 3 tbsp oil. Add hing. Add the ground dry masala.

6. Add the onion-ginger paste, cook till light brown and oil separates.

7. Add chopped tomatoes. Cook and mash till oil separates.

8. Add shredded ginger and sufficient water of boiled vegetables to get a thick gravy. Add amchoor, garam masala and salt to taste. Cook on low heat for 5-7 minutes.

9. Heat 2 tbsp oil separately in a pan. Add the 2 tsp reserved ground masala.

10. Immediately add the fried potato, boiled beans and carrot and ¼ tsp salt. Mix well for 2 minutes, so that masala coats the vegetables.

11. On a toothpick, insert a potato piece, then a bean and lastly a piece of carrot.

12. Make many such toothpicks and keep aside in an oven proof dish.

13. At serving time heat the prepared toothpicks in a hot oven for 4-5 minutes or microwave for a minute. Pour hot gravy on top and serve immediately.

Saunfiyaan Dhania Paneer

Serves 4

200 gms paneer - cut into 1" square pieces
2 tbsp cashewnuts (*kaju*) - soak in warm water for 10 minutes and grind to a paste
4 tbsp oil, 1 big onion - finely chopped
1" piece ginger and 8-10 flakes garlic - crushed to a paste or 2 tsp ginger-garlic paste
½ tsp red chilli powder, ½ tsp garam masala, 1 tsp salt, or to taste
1 tsp coriander (*dhania*) powder, 2 tbsp chopped fresh coriander, 1 cup milk

CORIANDER PASTE
¾ cup chopped fresh coriander, 2 green chillies, 1 tbsp fennel (*saunf*), ½ cup milk

1. Soak cashews in a little warm water for 10-15 minutes. Drain. Grind in a mixer blender to a very smooth paste using about 2 tbsp water.

2. Grind all the ingredients given under coriander paste to a thin paste in a mixer-grinder.

3. Heat 4 tbsp oil in a kadhai and add the chopped onions. Fry till golden.

4. Add the ginger-garlic paste, stir for few seconds.

5. Reduce heat, add the prepared coriander paste. Cook for 2 minutes.

6. On medium flame, add red chilli powder, garam masala, salt and coriander powder.

7. Add the prepared cashew paste. Mix well. Keep scraping sides if masala sticks to the sides/ bottom of the kadhai. Stir till masala leaves oil.

8. Add ½ cup of water. Boil, stirring at intervals. Remove from fire. Let the gravy cool down a little.

9. Add milk, mix well. Add paneer and return to fire and cook stirring continuously on low heat for 3- 4 minutes.

10. Serve hot, garnished with chopped coriander.

Papad ka Shak

Papads (spicy round wafers) and boondis (gram flour 'drops'), are available ready made. This mouth-watering vegetarian dish has no vegetables in it – an example of how the creative people of this dry land overcome the challenge of geography.

Serves 4

2 medium sized papads
1 cup yogurt (*dahi*), 1 tbsp gram flour (*besan*), ½ cup boondi
a pinch asafoetida (*hing*), ½ tsp cumin seeds
2-3 dry red chillies, ½ tsp red chilli powder, 1 tsp coriander powder
1 tsp garam masala, ¼ tsp turmeric (*haldi*) powder, ½ tsp salt, to taste
3 tbsp ghee/oil
1 tbsp green coriander - finely chopped

1. Roast papads & break into medium sized pieces.
2. Whisk together yogurt, gram flour and 1½ cups water till smooth.
3. Soak papad pieces & boondi in 2 cups hot water for 2-3 minutes. Strain & keep aside.
4. Heat oil. Add cumin seeds. When they turn golden, add asafoetida and broken red chillies. Fry for a minute or so.
5. Reduce heat. Add red chilli powder & whisked yogurt.
6. Add rest of the masalas & salt, stirring continuously.
7. As it begins to boil, add the papad & boondi.
8. Boil for a couple of minutes & garnish with chopped coriander leaves. Serve immediately.

Vegetable Korma

Serves 4

250 gms paneer - cut into 1" rectangular pieces and fried till golden
½ cup shelled peas (*matar*), 1 cup small florets of cauliflower
2 slices of tinned pineapple - cut into 1" pieces
2 small carrots - cut into round slices, 4-5 french beans - cut into ½" diagonal pieces
2 onions - chopped finely, 4 tbsp oil, ¼ tsp turmeric (*haldi*) powder
½ tsp garam masala, 2 tsp salt

GRIND TOGETHER (CASHEW-YOGURT PASTE)
4 tsp poppy seeds (*khus-khus*) - soaked in warm water for 30 minutes and drained
¾ cup yogurt (*haldi*), 2 tbsp cashewnuts (*kaju*), 2 tbsp grated coconut (fresh or desiccated)
2 whole dry red chillies, ½" piece ginger, 3-4 flakes garlic, 2 tsp saboot dhania
seeds of 2-3 green cardamom (*chhoti elaichi*)

1. Soak poppy seeds, cashewnuts, coconut, red chillies, ginger, garlic, coriander seeds and green cardamoms with little water. Keep aside for 15 minutes.
2. Drain and grind together to a paste along with yogurt. Keep aside the paste.
3. Cut paneer into 1" cubes and deep fry till golden. Deep fry cauliflower florets also.
4. Heat 4 tbsp oil. Add onions. Cook till onions turn golden. Add haldi. Stir to mix well.
5. Add the prepared cashew- yogurt paste. Cook on low heat for 3-4 minutes. Add beans, peas and carrots. Stir for 2 minutes. Add 1 cup water or enough to get a thick gravy. Boil.
6. Add garam masala and salt. Simmer for 5 minutes.
7. Add paneer, cauliflower and pineapple. Boil for 1 minute. Serve hot.

Dry & Masala

dry & masala

Nuggets in Onion Masala

Serves 4

1½ cups soya nuggets
1 green capsicum - cut into 1" square pieces
1 tomato - remove pulp and cut into 1" pieces
4 big onions - grind in a mixer to a paste
1 cup pureed tomatoes (puree about 3-4 tomatoes)
2 green chillies - finely chopped
1½ tsp salt or to taste
½ tsp red chilli powder or to taste
1 tsp garam masala powder
a pinch of cardamom (*chhoti elaichi*) powder
2 tbsp chopped fresh coriander
5 tbsp oil
3 tbsp malai or cream (optional)

1. Boil 4 cups water with 1 tsp salt. Add soya nuggets, give 2-3 boils. Remove from fire. Let it remain in hot water for 3-4 minutes. Strain and squeeze lightly.

2. Grind onions to a paste in a mixer.

3. Heat oil in a kadhai, add onion paste and cook on medium flame for 15 minutes, stirring continuously till the paste turns golden brown. Sprinkle a few drops of water if the masala sticks to the kadhai.

4. Add the tomato puree. Mix. Add green chillies, salt, red chilli powder, garam masala and cardamom powder. Cook for 10-12 minutes on medium heat.

5. Add the nuggets and cook for 4 minutes on medium fire.

6. Add capsicum and tomato pieces. Cook for 2 minutes.

7. Add ¼ cup water. Boil for 2 minutes on low heat.

8. Add garam masala, cardamom powder, malai or cream and coriander leaves. Mix well for 1 minute and serve hot.

Mili-Juli-Subzi

Serves 4

1 big potato - peeled, scooped to form small balls (about 12-13 balls)
200 gms (1 packet) baby cabbage or brussel sprouts (15-20 pieces) - trim the stalk end or
½ of a small cabbage - cut into 1" pieces
100 gms baby corn (7-8) - keep whole if small or cut into 2 pieces if big
¼ cup peas (*matar*)
6-7 French beans - cut into ¼" pieces (½ cup), 1 carrot - cut into ¼" pieces (½ cup)
12-15 baby onions or 4 regular onions of small size - cut into 4
15 cherry tomatoes or 2 regular small tomatoes - cut into 4, remove pulp
¼ tsp turmeric (*haldi*) powder , 1 tsp salt, ½ tsp red chilli powder
½ tsp garam masala, ½ tsp degi mirch

ONION PASTE
1 onion, 2 cloves (*laung*), seeds of 2 green cardamoms (*chhoti elaichi*)

TOMATO PASTE
¼ cup yogurt
2 tomatoes - put in boiling hot water for 3-4 minutes and peeled (blanched)

1. Make balls of a big potato with the help of a scooper.
2. Boil 7 cups water with 2 tsp salt. Add potato balls. Boil for 3 minutes. Add cabbage, baby corns, peas, beans and carrots. Boil for a minute. Remove from fire. Strain, put in cold water and strain again.
3. Heat 3 tbsp oil. Add onions. Saute for 2 min till soft. Add tomatoes. Stir.
4. Add all the vegetables. Sprinkle ½ tsp salt. Saute for 1 minute. Keep aside.
5. Grind all the ingredients of onion paste to a smooth paste. Keep aside.
6. Grind all the ingredients of tomato paste to a smooth paste. Keep aside.
7. For masala, heat 3 tbsp oil, add onion paste. Cook till light brown. Add haldi.
8. Add tomato paste. Stir for 5-10 minutes or till oil separates.
9. Add salt and red chilli powder. Cook till dry and oil separates.
10. Add ¾ cup water, ½ tsp garam masala and degi mirch. Cook for ½ a minute.
11. Add stir fried vegetables. Mix well for 2-3 minutes. Serve hot.

Hari Chutney Paneer

Chaatpata paneer dish which goes very well as a side dish.

Serves 4

200 gms paneer - cut into about 1" big triangular pieces of ¼" thickness
1½ cups of yogurt (*dahi*) - hang in a muslin cloth for 20 minutes
4 flakes garlic and ½" piece of ginger - crush to a paste or 1 tsp ginger-garlic paste
¼ tsp cumin seeds (*jeera*), 3 tbsp oil
1 onion - sliced thinly, ¾ tsp chaat masala - to sprinkle on paneer

CHUTNEY (GRIND TOGETHER)
½ cup poodina (*mint*), ½ cup green coriander
2 green chillies, 1 onion, ½ tsp black salt (*kala namak*)
½ tsp roasted cumin (*bhuna jeera*), ½ tsp salt or to taste, ¼ tsp powdered sugar

1. Hang yogurt in a muslin cloth for 20 minutes.

2. For chutney, wash coriander and mint leaves.

3. Grind together all the ingredients given under chutney to a paste. Keep the chutney aside.

4. Beat hung yogurt well till smooth.

5. To the hung yogurt, add the chutney. Keep aside.

6. Cut the block of paneer into rectangular slices of about ¼" thickness. Now cut each slice into 2 triangular pieces. Do not make the pieces too thick.

7. Cut each piece further into 2 triangles if the piece is big. Sprinkle chaat masala on the paneer. Mix gently.

8. Heat oil in a kadhai, add cumin and ginger- garlic paste. Cook for few seconds.

9. Add sliced onion and cook till golden.

10. Reduce heat and add the dahi-chutney. Cook for 2-3 minutes on low heat, stirring in between. Check salt. Keep aside.

11. At the time of serving, add paneer pieces to the chutney and mix gently but thoroughly to coat the pieces nicely with chutney. Heat on low fire. Serve.

Anjeeri Gobhi

Fried cauliflower, cooked in an anjeer flavoured masala. Something new, try it!

Serves 6

1 medium cauliflower (*gobhi*) - cut into medium size florets with long stalks
1 tsp cumin seeds (*jeera*), 2 onions - chopped, ¾" piece ginger- chopped
5 flakes garlic - chopped, 2 green chillies - deseeded and chopped

ANJEER PASTE

8 small figs (*anjeers*), 1 cup yogurt (*dahi*)
1 tsp garam masala, ¾ tsp red chilli powder, 1¾ tsp salt or to taste

TO SPRINKLE

2 small figs (*anjeers*) - chopped and roasted on a griddle (*tawa*)

1. Break the cauliflower into medium florets, keeping the stalk intact.

2. Heat 1 cup oil in a kadhai. Add all the cauliflower pieces and fry to a golden colour. Remove from oil and keep aside.

3. Churn all the ingredients given under anjeer paste in a mixer till smooth.

4. For masala, heat 2 tbsp oil in a kadhai. Add cumin. When it turns golden, add chopped onions. Stir till light brown.

5. Add chopped ginger, garlic and green chillies. Cook for a minute.

6. Add the prepared anjeer paste. Stir-fry for 2-3 minutes till the yogurt dries up a little. Keep aside till serving time.

7. Chop finely 2 figs and roast on a griddle till fragrant. Keep aside.

8. At serving time, heat the masala and add fried cauliflower. Mix well. Serve hot, sprinkled with roasted pieces of anjeer.

Achaari Bhindi

An unusual combination of bhindi in a masala flavoured with pickle spices.

Serves 4

½ kg lady's finger (*bhindi*)
4 big (300 gms) tomatoes - chopped finely, 2 tsp ginger or garlic paste, 15-20 curry leaves
½ tsp turmeric (*haldi*), ½ tsp red chilli powder, 1 tsp coriander (*dhania*) powder
¾ tsp salt, or to taste

ACHAARI SPICES
a pinch of asafoetida (*hing*), 1 tsp fennel (*saunf*), ½ tsp mustard seeds (*rai*)
½ tsp onion seeds (*kalaunji*), ¼ tsp fenugreek seeds (*methi daana*)

1. Wash lady's finger, wipe dry. Cut the tip of the head of each *bhindi*, leaving the pointed end as it is. Now cut bhindi vertically from middle making 2 smaller pieces from each *bhindi*. Heat oil in a kadhai and deep fry the bhindi on medium heat in 2 batches. Do not over fry the bhindi, it should retain it's green colour. Drain on a paper napkin. Keep aside.

2. Heat 2 tbsp oil and add ginger or garlic paste. Add curry patta and stir fry for a minute.

3. Add achaari spices. Stir till fenugreek seeds turns brown.

4. Add turmeric powder, chilli powder, coriander powder and salt. Stir for 30 seconds.

5. Add chopped tomatoes and stir for about 7-8 minutes or till oil separates.

6. Add fried bhindi. Sprinkle ¼ tsp salt, stir gently for few minutes till well mixed.

Tandoori Baby Corn Kibti

Whole baby corns coated with a yogurt marinade and grilled till golden.

Serves 4-5

200 gms thick baby corns - keep whole
juice of ½ lemon
1- 2 capsicums - cut into large 1" pieces
8 cherry tomatoes or 1 large tomato - cut into 8 pieces and pulp removed
1 onion - cut into fours and separated or 4 spring onions (keep white part whole)
1-2 tbsp melted butter for basting
some chaat masala - to sprinkle

MARINADE

1½ cups thick yogurt - hang for 30 minutes in a muslin cloth
1 tbsp thick ginger-garlic paste (squeeze out the liquid)
1 tbsp cornflour, 2 tbsp thick cream or malai
½ tsp black salt (*kala namak*), ¼ tsp turmeric (*haldi*) powder
¼ tsp carom seeds (*ajwain*)
1 tbsp tandoori or barbecue masala, ¼ tsp red chilli powder, ¾ tsp salt

1. Hang yogurt in a muslin cloth for ½ hour.

2. Boil 4-5 cups water with 2 tsp salt, ¼ tsp haldi and juice of ½ lemon. Add baby corns to boiling water. After the boil returns, boil for 1 minute only. Strain and wipe dry the corns on a clean kitchen towel. Keep aside.

3. Mix all ingredients of the marinade in a large bowl.

4. Rub oil generously on a wire rack or grill of the oven.

5. Add baby corns first to the marinade in the bowl and mix well to coat the marinade. Remove from bowl and arrange on the greased rack. In the remaining marinade in the bowl, add onion, capsicum and tomatoes. Leave these in the bowl itself. Marinate all for atleast ½ hour.

6. Grill baby corns first in an oven at 200°C for 15 minutes or roast in a gas tandoor. Pour a little melted butter on them to baste them, so that they keep moist. Put onion and capsicum also along with the corns and grill for 10 minutes. Lastly put the tomatoes in the oven with the onion-capsicum and grill further for 2-3 minutes.

7. Serve sprinkled with some chaat masala, along with lemon wedges.

NOTE:

If you do not want to do cook them in the oven, simply heat 2 tbsp oil in a kadhai. Add all the marinated vegetables in the hot oil and stir on high flame till coated well with the marinade and golden brown.

Subz Hyderabadi

A colourful curry of six different vegetables, creating a range of textures and flavours. Each vegetable is first fried separately and then mixed together and flavoured with aromatic spices.

Serves 6

2 potatoes - cut into ¾" pieces
2 medium carrots - cut into ¼" thick slices
12-15 French beans - cut into 1½" pieces, 10-12 medium florets of cauliflower
2 thin, long brinjals - cut into half lengthwise and then cut diagonally into 1½" pieces
¼ cup frozen or boiled peas
3 medium size onions - thinly sliced
1 tsp ginger paste, 1 tsp garlic paste
1 tsp salt, ¼ tsp turmeric powder, 1 tsp red chilli powder
1 cup yogurt (*dahi*) - whisked till very smooth, oil for frying

GRIND TOGETHER
2 green cardamoms (*chhoti elaichi*), 4 cloves (*laung*), 1 bay leaf (*tej patta*)
¼" piece of cinnamon (*dalchini*), ¼ tsp black cumin seeds (*shah jeera*)

1. Heat oil in a kadhai for deep frying. Deep fry potatoes on low medium heat till golden and almost cooked. Remove from oil. Add cauliflower and fry till light golden, for about 2 minutes. Add brinjals and deep fry till they start changing colour. Add the carrots and fry for just a minute to retain their colour. Similarly fry the beans for just a minute. Set aside.

2. Remove excess oil from the kadhai, leaving about 4 tbsp oil. Heat oil and add onions. Fry for 8-10 minutes till golden brown.

3. Reduce heat. Add ginger and garlic and fry for a minute. Add salt, turmeric and red chilli powder. Sprinkle 2-3 tbsp water and simmer for 2-3 minutes for the spices to blend well.

4. Keeping the heat to a minimum, add the fried vegetables and whisked yogurt. Stir and cook at medium-low heat, till the vegetables are fully cooked. Sprinkle a little water while cooking, if required.

5. Add the ground spices and mix well. Serve hot.

Phool Dilkhush

Pan fried whole cauliflowers coated with a delicious masala and topped with green peas.

Serves 4

2 very small whole cauliflowers, 2 tsp salt

MASALA

seeds of 1 black cardamom (*moti elaichi*), 3-4 peppercorns (*saboot kali mirch*)
2 cloves (*laung*), 3 tomatoes - roughly chopped, 1" ginger - chopped
3 onions - ground to a paste, 2 tbsp yogurt (*dahi*) - beat well till smooth
½ tsp red chilli powder
½ tsp garam masala, ½ tsp turmeric (*haldi*) powder, ½ tsp dry mango powder (*amchoor*)
½ tsp salt, or to taste, ¼ cup boiled peas - to garnish

1. Remove stems of cauliflowers. Boil 6 cups water with 2 tsp salt. Put the whole cauliflowers in it. When the water starts to boil again, remove from fire. Leave them in hot water for 10 minutes. Remove from water and refresh in cold water. Wipe dry on a clean kitchen towel.

2. Heat 5-6 tbsp oil in a large flat kadhai or a pan. Put both cauliflowers with flower side down in oil. Cover and cook on medium flame, stirring occasionally till the cauliflowers turn golden and get patches of dark brown colour here and there. Remove from oil. Keep aside.

3. Heat ½ tbsp oil in a clean kadhai. Add black cardamom, peppercorns and cloves. After a minute add chopped tomatoes and ginger. Cook for 4-5 minutes till they turn soft. Grind the cooked tomatoes to a paste. Keep aside.

4. Heat 3½ tbsp oil. Add onion paste. Cook till onions turn golden brown.

5.	Add above tomato paste. Cook for 4 minutes on low flame till masala turns dry.

6.	Add well beaten yogurt. Cook till masala turns reddish again.

7.	Reduce heat. Add red chilli powder, garam masala, turmeric powder, dry mango powder and salt. Cook for 1 minute. Add ¼ cup water to get a thick, dry masala. Boil. Cook for 1 minute on low flame. Remove from fire.

8.	Insert a little masala in between the florets of the fried cauliflower, especially from the backside.

9.	To serve, arrange the cauliflowers on a platter. Add ¼ cup water to the masala to make it a masala gravy. Boil. Add ½ tsp salt or to taste. Pour over the arranged cauliflowers. Heat in a microwave or a preheated oven. Alternately, heat the cauliflower in a kadhai in 1 tbsp oil at the time of serving. Heat the masala gravy separately. Arrange the heated cauliflowers on a serving platter. Pour the hot masala gravy over it. Sprinkle some boiled peas on it and on the sides.

Reshmi Paneer Masala

Serves 3-4

250 gms paneer - cut into 1½" cubes, 2 capsicums - cut into 1" pieces
2 onions - cut into 1" pieces, 3 tbsp gram flour (*besan*), 2 tbsp yogurt
1 tsp salt, ¼ tsp red chilli powder, 1 tbsp lemon juice, a few drops orange red colour
1 tbsp tomato puree, ½ tsp garam masala, 2 tbsp oil

GRIND TOGETHER TO A PASTE
1½" piece ginger, 3-4 flakes garlic, 1 tsp cumin seeds (*jeera*)
seeds of 2 green cardamoms (*chhoti elaichi*), 2 tbsp chopped coriander, 2-3 green chillies

1.	Grind garlic, ginger, cumin, green cardamoms, coriander and green chillies to a paste.

2.	Add gram flour, yogurt, salt, red chilli powder and lemon juice to the paste.

3.	Add enough orange colour to the paste to get a nice colour.

4.	Cut paneer into 1½" cubes. Put the paste in a big bowl and add the paneer pieces and mix well so as to coat the paste nicely on all the pieces. Add the onion and capsicum pieces also and mix lightly. Keep aside till serving time.

5.	Heat oil for frying. Pick up the paneer pieces and deep fry 2-3 paneer pieces at a time till slightly crisp. Keep aside till serving time. Also let the onion and capsicum be in the masala in the bowl and keep in the fridge.

6.	At the time of serving, heat 2 tbsp oil in a kadhai. Add onion and capsicum pieces and stir for a few minutes till onions turn soft and transparent. Add ¼ tsp salt. Add tomato puree and cook for a minute on low heat.

7.	Add paneer pieces. Sprinkle garam masala. Toss for a minute. Serve immediately.

Shimla Khumb Maskaawala

Serves 4

1 large capsicum - chopped

200 gms mushrooms - each cut into 4 pieces

1 tsp coriander seeds (*saboot dhania*) - crushed on a chakla-belan to split the seed into two

1 onion - chopped, 1 green chilli - deseeded and chopped

2 tbsp chopped fresh coriander

1 tsp salt, ½ tsp garam masala, ¼ tsp dry mango powder (*amchoor*)

a pinch of turmeric (*haldi*), a pinch of sugar, 1 tbsp oil, 2 tbsp butter

DAL-TOMATO PASTE

2 tbsp split bengal gram (*channa dal*)

1 tsp cumin (*jeera*), 2 tomatoes, ½ cup milk

1. Heat 1 tbsp oil in a pan or kadhai. Add mushrooms. Saute on high flame till golden. Add capsicums and saute for 1-2 minutes. Sprinkle ¼ tsp salt and ¼ tsp pepper. Remove from kadhai.

2. Boil 4 cups water with 1 tsp salt. Add channa dal. Boil covered on medium heat for about 5 minutes till dal turns soft. Add tomatoes to the boiling dal. Simmer covered for 2-3 minutes till the skin of the tomatoes starts to tear. Remove from fire. Strain. Peel tomatoes.

3. Blend blanched tomatoes, cooked dal and 1 tsp cumin with ½ cup milk to a smooth puree in a mixer-grinder. Keep dal-tomato paste aside.

4. Heat butter in a heavy bottomed kadhai. Add coriander seeds. Wait for 2 minutes till it starts turning brown.

5. When coriander seeds turns brown, add onion. Cook till onion turns golden. Add dal paste and stir well for 2 minutes.

6. Add green chilli, chopped coriander, salt, garam masala, dry mango powder, a pinch of turmeric and sugar. Bhuno for 3-4 minutes till dal turns dry. Stir continuously, scraping the dal sticking to the bottom and sides of the kadhai.

7. Add enough water, about 1½ cups, to get a thick masala gravy. Boil. Simmer on low heat for 2-3 minutes. Add mushrooms and capsicum. Mix well for 1 minute. Serve hot.

Besani Matar

A dry preparation of peas coated with gram flour and tossed with onion rings.

Serves 4

2 cups shelled peas - boiled or frozen, 3 tbsp oil, 1 tsp cumin seeds (*jeera*)
3 onions - cut into rings, ½" piece ginger - finely chopped
2 tbsp gram flour (*besan*), ¾ tsp garam masala, ½ tsp red chilli powder
1½ tsp coriander (*dhania*) powder, ¾ tsp salt or to taste
2 tbsp fresh coriander - chopped
2 tomatoes - puree in a mixer, 1 green chilli - deseeded & slit lengthwise, optional
1 tsp sesame seeds (*til*) - roasted on a tawa for 2 minutes till golden

1. Heat 3 tbsp oil in a kadhai, add cumin seeds. Let it turn golden. Add onion rings and stir till golden. Add ginger and saute over medium heat for ½ minute.

2. Add gram flour and saute on low heat for 2-3 minutes till gram flour turns fragrant.

3. Add pureed tomatoes, garam masala, red chilli powder and coriander powder. Saute for 3-4 minutes till puree turns dry. Add green chillies and coriander.

4. Add the boiled green peas and mix well. Add salt. Saute for 6-8 minutes. Transfer to a serving dish and sprinkle sesame seeds. Serve.

Dals & Other Pulses

dals & other pulses

Channa aur Dhingri Curry

An interesting dish to prepare with dry mushrooms (dhingri), when you find it difficult to decide a fresh vegetable.

Serves 6

100 gms (¾-1 cup approx.) Bengal gram (*kabuli channe*)
1 cup white dry mushrooms (*dhingri*)
6 tomatoes - grind to a puree
½ tsp turmeric (*haldi*), ½ tsp red chilli powder, 2 tsp coriander (*dhania*) powder
1 tbsp fenugreek leaves (*kasoori methi*) or 2-3 tbsp chopped fresh coriander
2 green chillies - deseeded and chopped finely
½ tsp garam masala, ½ tsp pepper, 1½ tsp salt, or to taste
5 tbsp ghee or oil

PASTE
4 onions, 10-15 flakes garlic, 1" piece ginger

1. Soak dhingri and channas separately overnight.

2. Wash dhingri very well in 2-3 changes of water, to remove dirt. Cut dhingri into small pieces, discarding the hard portions.

3. Pressure cook channas with salt and 2 cups water for about 20 minutes on low heat, after the pressure forms or till tender.

4. Grind ginger, garlic and onions to a paste.

5. Grind tomatoes to a puree.

6. Heat ghee. Add onion paste, fry till light brown.

7. Add turmeric powder, red chilli powder and coriander powder. Cook for a few seconds.

8. Add tomato puree, kasoori methi or coriander and green chillies. Cook till dry and ghee separates.

9. Strain channas reserving water. Add channas.

10. Add dhingri. Bhuno on medium fire for 4-5 minutes.

11. Add the channa water, garam masala, pepper and salt. Mix well. Cook on low flame for 8-10 minutes.

12. Serve hot, sprinkled with chopped coriander leaves.

Punjabi Rajmah

Servings 6

1½ cups red kidney beans (*lal rajmah*) - soaked overnight
1 tbsp split gram (*channe ki dal*) - soaked overnight
2½ tsp salt or to taste, 2 onions, 6-8 flakes garlic, 1" piece ginger
6 tbsp oil, 1 bay leaf (*tej patta*), 2 cloves (*laung*), 1 black cardamom (*moti elaichi*)
3 tomatoes - pureed in a blender, ½ cup yogurt - beaten well
¼ tsp turmeric (*haldi*) powder, 3 tsp coriander (*dhania*) powder
¼ tsp dry mango powder (*amchoor*), ½ tsp garam masala
1 tsp chilli powder, or to taste, 2 tbsp chopped fresh coriander

1. Pressure cook red kidney beans, split gram with salt together with about 10 cups water to give one whistle. Keep on low flame for 20 minutes. Remove from fire.

2. Grind onion, ginger and garlic to a paste.

3. Heat 5 tbsp oil in a heavy bottomed kadhai. Add bay leaf, black cardamom and cloves. Wait for 1 minute.

4. Add onion paste and stir fry till golden brown.

5. Reduce heat. Add turmeric powder, coriander powder, dry mango powder, garam masala and red chilli powder. Stir for a few seconds.

6. Add tomatoes pureed in a blender. Cook till tomatoes turn dry and oil separates.

7. Reduce heat. Add beaten yogurt and stir continuously on low flame till the masala turns red again and oil separates.

8. Strain and add the rajmahs, keeping the water aside. Stir fry on medium flame for 2-3 minutes, mashing occasionally.

9. Add the water of the rajmahs and pressure cook again for 8-10 minutes on low flame after the first whistle.

10. Remove from fire. Add freshly chopped coriander leaves. Serve hot with chappatis or boiled rice.

Special Sambhar

Serves 4

½ cup red gram dal (*arhar dal*) - soak for 30 minutes in 3 cups water
100 gms pumpkin (*kaddu*) or 2 brinjals (*baingan*) - any one vegetable of your choice
lemon sized ball of tamarind (*imli*), tiny piece of jaggery (*gur*)
a few coriander leaves, 1½ tsp salt or to taste, ¼ tsp turmeric (*haldi*) powder
¼ tsp asafoetida (*hing*) or 2 grains of asafoetida

POWDER

2 tsp coriander seeds (*saboot dhania*), ½ tsp cumin seeds (*jeera*)
½ tsp fenugreek seeds (*methi dana*), ¾ tsp split black gram (*dhuli urad ki dal*)
4-5 dry, whole red chillies, ½ tsp oil

TEMPERING (CHOWNK)

1 tbsp oil, ½ tsp mustard seeds (*sarson*), few curry leaves

1. Pressure cook dal with 3 cups of water to give 3 whistles till it turns soft. Mash slightly after the pressure drops. Keep aside.

2. To prepare powder, fry all the ingredients of the powder along with ½ tsp oil, on very low flame till the dal and fenugreek seeds changes colour. Grind to a fine powder. Keep aside.

3. Soak tamarind in ½ cup water. Boil. Remove from fire and add ½ cup water. Extract the juice. Add 1 more cup water to the left over imli and mash well. Extract more juice. Keep imli juice aside.

4. Put a heavy bottomed pan with 2 cups water on fire. Add the chopped vegetable, imli ka pani, salt and turmeric powder. Boil. Keep covered on fire for 8-10 minutes, till the vegetables get cooked.

5. Add cooked dal. Cover, simmer dal on low flame for 5 minutes, till every thing blends.

6. Add the prepared powder and hing.

7. Keep on flame for 2-3 minutes. Remove from fire and keep aside.

8. For chownk , heat 1 tbsp oil in a small pan. Add mustard seeds. When they splutters, add curry leaves. Remove from fire immediately and pour on the ready sambhar. Garnish with coriander leaves.

Dal Dakshini

Yellow dal with a South Indian tempering of imli and curry leaves.

Serves 4

¾ cup red gram lentils (*arhar ki dal*), ¼ cup split bengal gram (*channe ki dal*)
½ tsp turmeric (*haldi*) powder, 1½ tsp salt

TADKA

3 tbsp oil or ghee, 1 tsp cumin seeds (*jeera*), 1 tsp mustard seeds (*sarson*)
3-4 tbsp curry leaves, 1-2 dry, red chillies, 1 onion - chopped finely, 1 tsp ginger paste
1 tomato - pureed in a mixer, 1 tomato - chopped finely, 1 tsp coriander (*dhania*) powder
½ tsp garam masala, ¼ tsp red chilli powder, 1 tbsp imli pulp or juice of ½ lemon, or to taste
some chopped fresh coriander

1. Clean, wash dals. Add turmeric, salt & 3 cups of water. Pressure cook to give 1 whistle. Keep on low flame for 5 minutes. Remove from fire. Alternatively, boil in a pan till dal turns soft.

2. For the tadka, heat oil or ghee. Add cumin and mustard seeds. Let cumin turn golden.

3. Add curry leaves and dry red chillies. Add onion and cook till light golden. Add ginger paste. Stir for a minute.

4. Add freshly pureed tomato. Cook till tomato turns dry. Add chopped tomato and cook for 2-3 minutes till soft.

5. Add masalas – coriander powder, garam masala and red chilli powder. Stir for 2 minutes on low heat. Add imli pulp or juice of ½ lemon. Mix well and pour on the cooked dal. Mix lightly and serve sprinkled with some coriander.

Pindi Chhole

Serves 4

PRESSURE COOK TOGETHER
1 cup Bengal gram (*channa kabuli*)
2 tbsp split gram (*channe ki dal*)
2 black cardamoms (*moti elaichi*), 1" stick cinnamon (*dalchini*)
2 tsp tea leaves tied in a muslin cloth or 2 tea bags

MASALA
2 onions - chopped finely
1½ tsp pomegranate seeds (*anaardana*) powder
3 tomatoes - chopped finely
1" piece ginger - chopped finely
1 green chilli - chopped finely
1 tsp coriander (*dhania*) powder, ½ tsp garam masala
½ tsp red chilli powder or to taste
1 tsp channa masala, 1¼ tsp salt or to taste

1. Soak channa and channe ki dal overnight or for 6-8 hours in a pressure cooker. Next morning, discard water. Wash channas with fresh water and add black cardamoms, cinnamon, tea leaves, ¼ tsp soda and enough water to cover the channas nicely.

2. Pressure cook all the ingredients together to give one whistle. After the first whistle, keep on low flame for about 20-25 minutes. Keep aside.

3. Heat 4 tbsp oil. Add onions. Saute till transparent. Add pomegranate seeds powder. Cook stirring till onions turn brown. (Do not burn them).

4. Add chopped tomatoes, ginger and green chill. Stir fry for 3-4 minutes.

5. Add coriander powder, garam masala and chilli powder. Mash and stir fry tomatoes occasionally till they turn brownish in colour and oil separates.

6. Strain channas, reserving the liquid. Remove tea bag from the boiled channas.

7. Add the strained channas to the onion-tomato masala. Mix well.

8. Add salt. Stir fry gently for 5-7 minutes.

9. Add channa masala and salt. Add the channa liquid. Cook for 15-20 minutes on medium heat till the liquid dries up a little.

10. Serve garnished with onion rings, green chillies and tomato wedges.

Dal Kofta Curry

Makes 12-15 koftas

KOFTA

¾ cup *arhar ki dal* - soaked for at least 2 hours

1" piece ginger, 4-5 flakes garlic, 3-4 green chillies

¼ cup chopped fresh coriander

½ tsp garam masala, ½ tsp red chilli powder, ½ tsp salt, or to taste

¾ tsp Eno fruit salt

CURRY

½ tsp cumin seeds (*jeera*), 2 black cardamoms (*moti elaichi*), 3-4 cloves (*laung*)

8-10 curry leaves, ½ tsp red chilli powder

2 medium tomatoes - pureed and strained

some chopped coriander for garnishing

MIX TOGETHER

1 cup yogurt, 2 tsp gram flour (*besan*), ½ tsp turmeric (*haldi*) powder

1½ tsp salt, 1 tsp ginger-garlic paste

1. Wash and soak the dal for 2 hours or more. Drain water. Grind to a coarse (rough) paste along with ginger, garlic and green chillies. Mix garam masala, red chilli powder, salt and coriander leaves to the dal paste.

2. Add Eno fruit salt and beat well for 3-4 minutes till light. Make balls.

3. Boil 1½ cups water in a pressure cooker. Grease an idli stand and place balls of dal paste on it. Close the cooker without the weight and steam for 7-8 minutes on medium heat. Remove from fire and keep aside.

4. For the curry, mix together yogurt, gram flour, turmeric, salt, ginger-garlic paste.

5. Add 1 cup water. Beat well till really smooth.

6. Heat 3 tbsp oil. Add cumin, black cardamoms and cloves. Wait till cumin turns golden.

7. Add curry leaves. Add red chilli powder and immediately add the yogurt mixture. Stir till it boils.

8. Add pureed tomatoes. Give 2-3 boils.

9. Add koftas. Cover, lower heat. Simmer for 4-5 minutes.

10. Serve hot garnished with fresh coriander.

Tadka Dal

Serves 4

¼ cup *channa dal*, ½ cup *dhuli masoor*, ¼ cup *dhuli urad dal*

TADKA

½ tsp fennel (*saunf*), ¼ tsp mustard seeds (*sarson*), ¼ tsp onion seeds (*kalaunji*)
¼ tsp cumin, ¼ tsp fenugreek seeds (*methi dana*)
1 onion - finely chopped, 1 tomato - chopped finely
4-5 flakes garlic - crushed, 1" piece ginger - chopped finely
½ tsp each of coriander (*dhania*) powder and garam masala
¼ tsp dry mango powder (*amchoor*), 2 tbsp chopped fresh coriander

1. Wash all dals together in a pressure cooker. Add 3½ cups water, 1 tsp salt and ¼ tsp turmeric powder. Pressure cook to give 1 whistle and then keep on low flame for 2-3 minutes. Remove from fire and let the pressure drop by itself.

2. Heat 3 tbsp oil. Add all together - fennel seeds, mustard seeds, onion seeds, cumin seeds and fenugreek seeds.

3. When fenugreek seeds turns golden, add onions. Cook till golden.

4. Add garlic and ginger. Stir. Add tomato. Add ½ tsp coriander, ½ tsp garam masala and ¼ tsp dry mango powder. Cook for 3-4 minutes till tomatoes are well blended.

5. Pour on the cooked dal. Garnish with chopped coriander.

Dal Makhani

Serves 4-5

1 cup whole black beans (*urad saboot*)

2 tbsp desi ghee

1½ tsp salt, 5 cups of water

1 cup ready made tomato puree

¼ tsp nutmeg (*jaiphal*) powder, ½ tsp garam masala

1½ tbsp dry fenugreek leaves (*kasoori methi*)

2-3 tbsp butter, preferably white

GRIND TO A PASTE

2 dry, whole red chillies, preferably Kashmiri red chillies - deseeded & soaked for 10 minutes and then drained

1" piece ginger, 6-8 flakes garlic

ADD LATER

½ cup milk mixed with ½ cup cream

1. Wash the dal, and soak in warm water for atleast 2-3 hours.

2. Drain water. Wash several times in fresh water, rubbing well, till the water no longer remains black.

3. Pressure cook dal with 5 cups water, 2 tbsp ghee, salt and ginger-garlic-chilli paste. After the first whistle, keep on low flame for 30 minutes. Remove from fire.

4. After the pressure drops, mash the hot dal a little. Keep aside.

5. To the dal in the cooker, add tomato puree, fenugreek leaves, garam masala and nutmeg powder.

6. Add butter. Simmer on medium flame for 30 minutes, stirring dal occasionally. Remove from fire. Keep aside to cool till the time of serving.

7. At the time of serving, add milk mixed with cream to the dal. Keep dal on fire and bring to a boil on low heat, stirring constantly. Mix very well with a *karchhi*. Simmer for 2 minutes more, to get the right colour and smoothness. Remove from fire. Serve.

NOTE:

Originally the dal was cooked by leaving it overnight on the burning coal angithis. The longer the dal simmered, the better it tasted.

Sukhi Urad ki Dal

Serves 4

1 cup split black beans (*urad dhuli dal*) - soaked for ½ hour
½" piece ginger - very finely chopped, 2 green chillies - very finely chopped
½ tsp turmeric (*haldi*) powder, 1¼ tsp salt, 1 cup water

TADKA/TEMPERING

3-4 tbsp desi ghee or oil, 1 big onion - finely chopped
1" piece ginger - cut into match sticks, 1 big tomato - finely chopped
½ tsp chilli powder, ½ tsp garam masala, 2 tbsp chopped coriander leaves to garnish

1. Clean, wash dal. Soak dal in water for ½ hour. Strain dal.
2. Pressure cook dal with 1 cup water and all the other ingredients. When the first whistle comes, slow down the fire and keep for 1 minute only.
3. Remove from fire. Open the cooker only after the pressure drops down. Keep aside.
4. At the time of serving, for the tempering, heat ghee. Add onions. Cook till light brown.
5. Add ginger match sticks and stir for a few seconds till onions turn brown.
6. Add tomatoes. Cook for 2-3 minutes.
7. Add ½ tsp chilli powder and ½ tsp garam masala. Cook for ½ minute.
8. Pour the hot oil or ghee over the dal. Mix gently.
9. Serve hot sprinkled with chopped coriander.

Arhar with Paalak

Serves 4

3 cups (250 gms) chopped spinach (*paalak*), 1 cup red gram dal (*arhar dal* or *toovar ki dal*)
1 small flake garlic - finely chopped (optional)
½" piece ginger - finely chopped, 1 green chilli - finely chopped
½ tsp turmeric (*haldi*) powder, 1½ tsp salt, or to taste, 1 tsp oil

TADKA

3 tbsp ghee, 1 tsp cumin (*jeera*), 1 onion - chopped, 1 tomato - chopped
½ tsp coriander (*dhania*) powder, ¼ tsp dry mango powder (*amchoor*)
½ tsp garam masala, ½ tsp red chilli powder

1. Pick, clean and wash dal. Wash chopped spinach in plenty of water.

2. Mix spinach, dal, garlic, ginger, green chilli, turmeric powder, salt and 1 tsp oil. Add 3 cups water to the dal. Pressure cook dal to give one whistle and then keep on low flame for 6-7 minutes. Remove from fire.

3. For tadka, heat ghee in a kadhai. Reduce heat and add cumin. Let it turn golden brown. Add the onion and cook on low heat till it becomes dark brown, but be careful not to burn it. Add tomatoes and cook for 2-3 minutes on low flame.

4. Add coriander powder, dry mango powder and garam masala. Cook for ½ minute.

5. Remove from fire, add red chilli powder. Mix. Pour over the hot dal. Mix gently.

Rice & Roti

rice & roti

Panchratan Chaawal

Serves 6-8

2 cups rice - boiled to get 5-6 cups boiled rice
12-15 cashewnuts (*kaju*), 12-15 raisins (*kishmish*)
2 onions - sliced
½ cup paneer - cut into tiny cubes
1 cup boiled green peas
½ cup boiled and diced carrots (cut into small cubes)
½ of an apple or 2 rings of tinned pineapple - cut into ½" pieces
1 tsp black cumin seeds (*shah-jeera*)
2 sticks cinnamon (*dalchini*), 2 cloves (*laung*), 3 black cardamoms (*moti elaichi*)
¼ tsp saffron (*kesar*) - soaked in 1 tbsp water or a few drops orange colour
4 tbsp ghee/oil, 1½ tsp salt or to taste

PASTE
4 flakes garlic, 1" piece ginger
4 green chillies

1. Boil the rice in plenty of water (about 10 cups) in a large pan. Each grain of the cooked rice should be separate. Drain and spread out in a broad tray for 1 hour.

2. Grind garlic, ginger and green chillies to a paste.

3. Heat the ghee and fry the cashewnuts to a golden colour. Remove from ghee and keep aside.

4. Reduce flame and add the raisins in the same ghee. Remove after a few seconds when they swell and keep aside.

5. In the same kadhai, add sliced onions, fry till golden brown and crisp. Remove from ghee and keep aside.

6. Add the black cumin, cinnamon, cloves and cardamoms to the remaining ghee, fry for a few seconds.

7. Add the prepared garlic-ginger paste. Cook on low flame for ½ minute.

8. Add paneer, green peas, carrots, pineapple, salt and mix well. Stir fry for 2 minutes.

9. Add the rice. Stir fry till well mixed.

10. Rub the kesar strands to extract colour and add to the rice along with the water or sprinkle drops of colour. Stir fry well to colour the rice partly. Decorate with fried cashewnuts, raisins and crisp browned onions.

Bisi Bele Bhath

Eleven ingredients make up the complex taste of the Bisi Bele Spice paste. Rice and dal are cooked together with a variety of vegetables – a strongly flavoured, hearty and satisfying traditional dish.

Serves 4-6

1 cup rice

1 cup *arhar dal* - soaked for 15 minutes

1 small carrot - cut into small pieces, 1 potato - cut into small pieces

5-6 beans - cut into small pieces

1 long, thin brinjal - cut into small pieces

1 drumstick - cut into small pieces

a pinch asafoetida (*hing*), 1 tsp mustard seed (*sarson*)

2-3 dry red chillies, 15-20 curry leaves, 2 green chillies - cut into small pieces

1 large onion - cut into small pieces, a pinch of turmeric (*haldi*) powder

2 lemon size tamarind (*imli*) soaked in ¾ cup water - strained to get 1 cup pulp

2 tsp sugar or jaggery (*gur*)

BISI BELE PASTE

2 tbsp *channa dal*, 2 tbsp *dhuli urad dal*

pinch of asafoetida (*hing*), 2 tbsp coriander seeds (*saboot dhania*)

4-6 dry red chillies, 1 tsp cumin seeds (*jeera*), 1 tsp fenugreek seeds (*methi danna*)

1 tsp mustard seeds (*rai*), 4 black peppercorns (*saboot kali mirch*)

2 stick cinnamon (*dalchini*), 2 tbsp dried grated coconut (*kopra*)

TOPPING

1 tbsp ghee and a few curry leaves

1. To make the Bisi bele paste, heat a pan and dry roast channa and urad dal till brown. Remove from heat. In the same pan add 1 tsp oil and add asafoetida, coriander seeds, cumin seeds, mustard seeds, fenugreek seeds, black pepper, red chillies and cinnamon. Cook till cumin seeds and fenugreek turn light brown, add coconut and stir for ½ minute. Remove from heat. Place the roasted dals in a grinder and grind to a smooth powder, now add the rest of the roasted ingredients in the grinder and grind all using about ½ cup water to get a smooth paste.

2. For bhath, add rice, dal and 6 cups of water in a cooker. Add 3 tsp salt . Pressure cook to 1 whistle. Lower heat and cook for 3-4 minutes. Remove from heat. Let pressure drop by itself.

3. Heat 6 tbsp oil in kadhai, add a pinch of asafoetida, add mustard seeds, broken red chillies, curry leaves and green chillies. Stir and add the onions. Cook till slightly soft. Add the vegetables and lower heat. Cover and cook for about 10 minutes or till vegetables are soft, add a pinch of turmeric and the bisi bele paste. Stir well. Remove from heat.

4. Open the cooker, add the vegetables to the cooked rice-dal mixture, mix lightly.

5. Mash soaked imli. Strain to get a puree, add to the bhath and mix. Add sugar.

6. Add ghee and curry patta. Serve hot with potato chips or masala boondi or raita.

Dum Hyderabadi Biryani

Serves 6

RICE
2 cups (250 gms) basmati rice - washed and kept in the strainer for 30 minutes
4-5 green cardamom (*chhoti elaichi*), 2 bay leaves (*tej patta*), 5-6 cloves (*laung*)
3 tsp salt, 1 tbsp lemon juice, 10 cups water

VEGETABLES
2 thin carrots - peeled and cut into round slices, 20 french beans - cut into ¼" pieces
½ of a small cauliflower - cut into small florets

MIX TOGETHER
1½ cups yogurt, 1 tbsp mint - chopped finely, 1 tbsp coriander - chopped finely
2-3 drops kewra essence or ½ tsp ruh kewra, ½ tsp salt

CRUSHED SPICES TOGETHER
½ tsp black cumin (*shah jeera*), 3-4 blades mace (*javetri*)
seeds of 1 black cardamom (*moti elaichi*), 1 stick of cinnamon (*dalchini*)

TO SEAL
aluminium foil and dough

OTHER INGREDIENTS
4-5 tbsp melted ghee or oil
8-10 almonds (*badam*) - split into two pieces, 1 tbsp raisins (*kishmish*)
2 large onion - sliced, 3 tsp ginger-garlic paste, 1 tsp red chilli powder, 1½ tsp salt
a few mint leaves (*poodina*), orange and yellow colour
seeds of 4 green cardamom (*chhoti elaichi*) - crushed to a powder, 1 tbsp melted ghee

1. Wash rice several times. Strain. Let it be in the strainer for 30 minutes. (Do not soak).

2. Boil 10 cups water with all ingredients given under rice - green cardamoms, cloves, bay leave, salt and lemon juice.

3. When the water boils, throw in the rice. Stir. Boil just for 4-5 minutes so that the rice is a little chewy and not fully soft.

4. Remove from fire. If you find the grains too hard, let them be in hot water for 2 minutes. Strain in a big steel strainer or a colander. Run a fork frequently in the rice to separate the grains of rice. Let the rice be in the strainer for 10 minutes to drain out all the water. Now spread rice in a big tray on a cloth. Keep under the fan for 10 minutes. Remove whole spices from the cooked rice and discard them.

5. Heat ghee or oil. Add almonds and raisins. Stir for a few seconds. Remove from oil and keep aside for topping.

6. Add onions and stir till rich brown. Remove half onion and keep aside for garnish. Reduce heat. Add crushed spices, ginger-garlic paste, chilli powder and salt. Mix.

7. Add vegetables and stir for 2 minutes.

8. Reduce heat. Add ½ of the yogurt mixture leaving some to put on rice later on.

9. Stir to mix. Cook, stirring on low heat till the vegetables are just done or crisp-tender. Do not over cook. After the vegetables are done, a little masala, about ¼ cup should remain (semi dry). If the vegetables turn too dry, add ¼ cup water. Boil. Remove from fire.

10. To assemble the biryani, take a *handi* or a baking dish. Grease it. Spread 1/3 of the rice in the dish. Spoon some yogurt on the rice.

11. Sprinkle yellow colour on half of the rice & orange colour on the other half of the rice.

12. Spread half of the vegetables over the rice. Put ½ the rice on the vegetables. Spoon ½ of the yogurt mix on the rice. Sprinkle colours. Do not mix.

13. Repeat vegetable layer using all the vegetable.

14. Spread remaining rice. Spoon yogurt on it. Sprinkle colours. Do not mix.

15. Sprinkle cardamom powder and 1 tbsp of melted ghee over the rice. Put a few mint leaves on the rice.

16. Sprinkle browned onions, almonds and raisins. Cover with foil.

17. Take a big ball of atta dough, roll in into a long strip.

18. Cover the *handi* with a foil nicely, pressing the edges well. Seal the end of the *handi* by pressing the dough strip on the foil, sticking it with the *handi*.

19. Keep in the oven, if using a glass dish, for 'dum' at 150°C for 30 minutes or keep on a tawa, if using a metal *handi*, on very low heat for 15-20 minutes.

Tandoori Platter with BBQ Sauce

Serves 8

250 gms paneer - cut into large (1½") cubes, 2 capsicums - cut into large cubes
200 gms (10-12) mushrooms - trim ends of the stalks, leaving them whole
100 gms baby corns - blanched with a pinch of turmeric powder & 1 tsp salt in 3 cups water
8 cherry tomatoes or 1 large tomato - cut into 8 pieces and pulp removed
1 onion - cut into fours and separated

MARINADE

1 cup thick yogurt - hang for 30 minutes in a muslin cloth, 2 tbsp thick cream
2 tbsp oil, 1 tbsp cornflour, 1 tbsp thick ginger-garlic paste, ½ tsp black salt (*kala namak*)
¼ tsp turmeric (*haldi*) powder or tandoori red colour, 2 tsp tandoori masala
½ tsp red chilli powder, ¾ tsp salt or to taste

BARBECUE SAUCE

3 tbsp butter or oil, 4-5 flakes garlic - crushed, 2 large tomatoes - pureed till smooth
¼ cup ready made tomato puree, ¼ tsp red chilli powder, ½ tsp pepper, ¾ tsp salt or to taste
¼ tsp sugar, ½ tsp worcestershire sauce, ½ tsp soya sauce

RICE

1 cup uncooked rice - soaked for 1 hour, 1 tbsp sugar
2 tbsp oil, ½ tsp cumin seeds (*jeera*), 2 small onions - sliced finely
1" stick cinnamon (*dalchini*), 2 bay leaves (*tej patta*), 2 cloves (*laung*)
2 green cardamoms (*chhoti elaichi*), 3-4 peppercorns (*saboot kali mirch*), 1 tsp salt or to taste

1. For the marinade, hang yogurt in a muslin cloth for ½ hour.

2. For rice, mix sugar with 3 tbsp water in a small heavy bottomed vessel. Cook on low flame till it is rich brown in colour. Add two cups of hot water to it. Stir till dissolved. Remove from fire and keep aside.

3. Heat oil. Add cumin. When it turns golden add onions and stir fry till golden brown in colour. Add all whole masalas.

4. Drain rice. Add rice to onions. Fry gently for 1-2 minutes. Add caramel sugar water and salt. Cover and cook on a very low fire till the water gets absorbed and the rice is done. Keep aside.

5. For vegetables, rub oil generously on a wire rack or grill of the oven.

6. Mix all ingredients of the marinade. Add paneer, mushrooms and baby corns to the marinade and mix well to coat the marinade. Remove from bowl and arrange on the rack or on greased wooden skewers. In the remaining marinade which is sticking to the sides of the bowl, add onion, capsicum and tomatoes. Leave these in the bowl itself. Marinate all for atleast ½ hour.

7. Grill paneer and vegetables in the oven at 210°C/410°F for 12-15 minutes or roast in a gas tandoor, on the wire rack or on skewers. Spoon a little oil/melted butter (basting) on them. Add onion, capsicum and tomatoes. Grill for another 5-7 minutes.

8. For the sauce, heat oil in a kadhai. Add garlic and cook till light brown.

9. Add fresh tomato puree, ready made tomato puree and chilli powder. Cook for 5 minutes till well blended. Add all other ingredients and ½ cup water to get a thin sauce. Boil. Simmer for 2 minutes. Remove from fire and keep aside.

10. To serve, heat rice separately in a microwave or an oven. Spread the rice on a serving plate. Put some hot sauce on the rice. Arrange grilled vegetables. Pour some hot sauce over the vegetables. Serve the extra sauce in a separate sauce boat or bowl. Serve at once.

Khasta Roti

Makes 4-5

1 cup semolina (*suji*), ¼ cup plain flour (*maida*)
a pinch of carom seeds (*ajwain*), a pinch of fennel (*saunf*)

OTHER INGREDIENTS
½ tsp salt, ½ tsp sugar
½ cup warm milk, 1 tsp ghee - melted

1. Sieve the flour and semolina in a paraat, put saunf and carom seeds in it.
2. Dissolve salt and sugar in milk.
3. Make a bay in the sieved flour. Pour milk and mix it gradually. Knead it to make a dough. Cover with a moist cloth for 10-15 minutes and keep aside.
4. Add melted ghee and mix gradually, kneading it well.
5. Divide the dough into 12 equal portions, make balls, cover and keep aside.
6. Flatten each ball with a rolling pin and roll to a slightly thick roti. Prick the entire roti with a fork. Cook carefully in a heated tandoor till light brown specs appear.

Nan Badaami

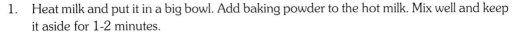

Makes 6

2½ cups (250 gms) plain flour (*maida*)
½ cup hot milk, 1 tsp baking powder
½ cup warm water (approx.)
½ tsp salt
10 almonds (*badaam*) - cut into long thin pieces (slivered)

1. Heat milk and put it in a big bowl. Add baking powder to the hot milk. Mix well and keep it aside for 1-2 minutes.
2. Sift flour and salt together. Add flour to the hot milk. Mix.
3. Knead to a dough with enough warm water.
4. Keep in a warm place for 3-4 hours.
5. Make 6-8 balls.
6. Roll out each ball to an oblong shape. Spread ghee all over. Fold one side (lengthways) a little, so as to overlap an inch of the nan. Press on the joint with the rolling pin (*belan*).
7. Sprinkle some chopped almonds. Press with a rolling pin (*belan*). Pull one side of the nan to give it a pointed end like the shape of the nan.
8. Apply some water on the back side of the nan. Stick in a hot tandoor.
9. Cook till nan is ready. Spread butter on the ready nan and serve hot.

Makki ki Roti

Makes 6-7

2 cups maize flour (*makki ka atta*), hot water - to knead, ghee for frying

1. Sieve the flour. Knead gently with hot water to a soft dough. Do not knead the dough too much in advance.
2. Tear an old polythene bag into two halves. Keep one piece of polythene on the rolling platform (*chakla*). Put one ball of the kneaded dough on the polythene. Cover with the other piece of polythene, such that there is a plastic cover above and beneath the ball.
3. Roll carefully to a slightly thick roti.
4. Cook roti on both sides on a tawa. Add some ghee and fry both sides on low flame. Serve hot with sarson ka saag.

Tandoori Roti

Makes 6-7

2 ½ cups whole wheat flour (*atta*)
1 cup water (approx.), ½ tsp salt, 2-3 tbsp ghee

1. Keep ghee in the fridge for some time, so that it solidifies.
2. Make a soft dough with whole wheat flour, salt and water. Keep aside for half an hour.
3. Divide the dough into 6 equal balls. Flatten each ball, roll out each into a round of 5" diameter.
4. Spread 1 tsp of solidified ghee. Sprinkle a teaspoon of dry flour on the ghee.
5. Make a slit, starting from any one end till almost to the other end, leaving just 1".
6. Start rolling from the slit, to form an even cone. Roll out, to a diameter of 5", applying pressure only at the centre and not on the sides. Cook carefully in a heated tandoor till brown specs appear.

Bhature

Makes 8

2 cups plain flour (*maida*)
1 cup semolina (*suji*)
½ tsp soda-bicarb, ½ tsp salt, ½ tsp sugar
½ cup sour yogurt, oil for deep frying

1. Soak semolina in water, which is just enough to cover it. Keep aside for 10 minutes.
2. Sift salt, soda and flour in a paraat. Add sugar, soaked semolina and yogurt.
3. Knead with enough warm water to make a dough of rolling consistency.
4. Knead again with greased hands till the dough is smooth.
5. Brush the dough with oil. Keep the dough in a greased polythene and keep it in a warm place for 3-4 hours.
6. Make 8-10 balls. Roll each ball to an oblong shape. Deep fry in hot oil. Serve.

Poodina Parantha

Makes 6

4 tbsp freshly chopped or dry mint leaves (*poodina*)
2 cups whole wheat flour (*atta*)
1 tsp carom seeds (*ajwain*)
2 tbsp oil
½ tsp salt
½ tsp red chilli powder

1. Mix atta with all ingredients except mint. Add enough water to make a dough of rolling consistency.
2. Make walnut sized balls. Roll out to make a thick chappati.
3. Spread 1 tsp of ghee all over. Cut a slit from the outer edge till the centre.
4. Start rolling from the slit to form a cone.
5. Keeping the cone upright, press cone gently.
6. Roll out to a thick roti. Sprinkle poodina. Press with the rolling pin (*belan*).
7. Cook on a tawa, frying on both sides or apply some water on the back side of the parantha and stick it in a hot tandoor. Serve hot.

Lemon Rice

Serves 4

1 cup uncooked rice - soaked in 1¼ cups water for ½ hour in a pressure cooker
3 tbsp oil

MIX TOGETHER

juice of 2 lemons, 1" piece ginger - cut into match sticks

TADKA

a pinch of asafoetida (*hing*), ½ tsp mustard seeds (*sarson*)
½ tsp split black beans (*dhuli urad dal*), ½ tsp split bengal gram (*channa dal*)
2 whole, dry red chillies, ½ tsp turmeric (*haldi*) powder, ½ tsp salt, 15 curry leaves

1. Add 1 tsp oil to the soaked rice in the pressure cooker and keep on fire. Remove from fire as soon as it is about to give a whistle. Let the pressure drop by itself and let the rice cool down. Alternatively, boil rice in a large pan with plenty of water.

2. When cool, spread it out in a large plate or tray. Sprinkle 1 tbsp oil on the rice and mix gently with a fork.

3. Mix together the ginger pieces and lemon juice. Keep aside.

4. For tadka, heat a small kadhai and add 1 tbsp oil. Add asafoetida, mustard seeds, urad dal, channa dal, red chillies, turmeric powder and salt.

5. In the end, add the curry leaves and put off the flame.

6. Mix for 1 minute and turn the oil in the kadhai on to the rice spread out in a tray.

7. Add the lemon juice along with the ginger pieces also and mix thoroughly till everything blends well. Serve hot.

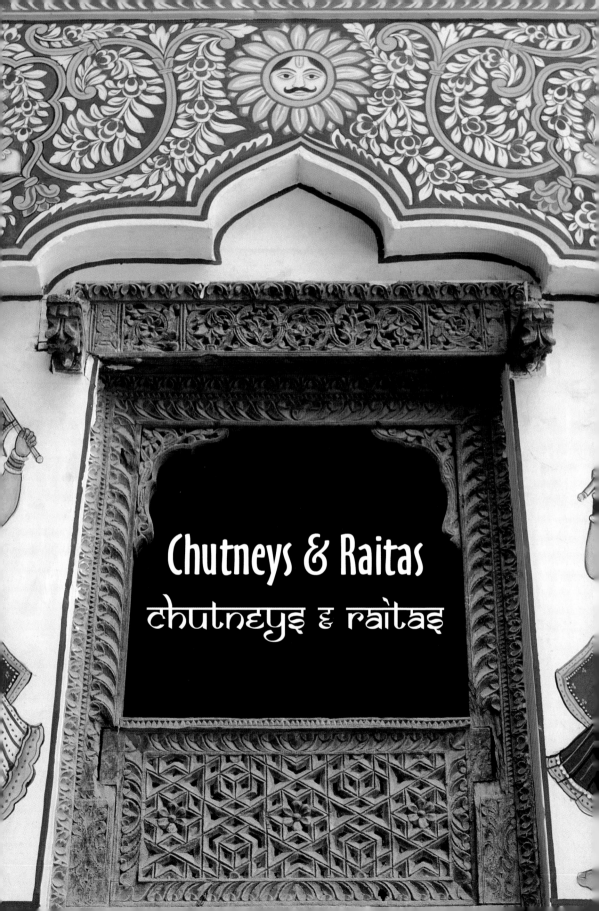

Chutneys & Raitas
chutneys & raitas

Raita Anaarkali

A sweet & sour raita with fresh kernels of pomegranate. Slices of boiled potatoes are arranged around the yogurt. The tamarind chutney is very simple to prepare & it can be stored for many days in the freezer. You may have this raita even without the tamarind chutney.

Serves 4-6

500 gms yogurt (2½ cups), 1 cup pomegranate kernels - (*anaar ke daane*)
½ tsp red chilli powder, ½ tsp salt or to taste, 1 tsp ground roasted cumin (*bhuna jeera*)
2 small potatoes - boiled and cut into slices, a few fresh coriander leaves - to garnish
1 tbsp tamarind (*imli*) chutney

TAMARIND (IMLI) CHUTNEY

1 tbsp tamarind pulp (a small ball of imli, boiled with ¼ cup of water and strained to get pulp)
3 tbsp sugar, or to taste, ½ cup water, ½ tsp ground ginger (*sonth*), optional
¼ tsp black salt, salt or to taste, ½ tsp ground, roasted cumin (*bhuna jeera*) powder

1. Mix all ingredients of the tamarind chutney. Keep on heat and stir well to mix. Cook till a saucy consistency is reached. Cool. The chutney will thicken as it cools.
2. Beat the yogurt well till absolutely smooth. Add pomegranate kernels, salt, red chilli powder and roasted cumin powder to the beaten yogurt. Transfer to a serving dish. Surround the dish with boiled potato circles.
3. Pour a little chutney on the potatoes slices. Arrange a small bunch of whole coriander leaves in the centre. Garnish with kernels of pomegranate.

Peanut- Raisin Raita

Serves 4-5

500 gms yogurt (2½ cups)
¼ cup roasted peanuts (*moongphali*), 2 tbsp raisins (*kishmish*)
½ tsp coriander (*dhania*) powder
½ tsp roasted cumin (*bhuna jeera*) powder, 1 tbsp chopped fresh coriander
salt and red chilli powder to taste

1. Beat yogurt well, till smooth.
2. Add all the ingredients to the yogurt. Mix well. Keep in the fridge till serving time.

Baghara Raita

Servings 4-5

½ kg yogurt - 2½ cups, salt to taste
½ cup grated coconut, 1 cup shredded cabbage
¼" piece ginger - grated finely, 2 green chillies - chopped finely

BAGHAR

1 tbsp oil, ½ tsp mustard seeds (*sarson*), ½ tsp cumin seeds (*jeera*)

1. Beat yogurt, add cabbage, coconut, ginger, green chillies and salt.
2. Heat 1 tbsp oil and add cumin and mustard seeds. Wait for ½ a minute and pour over the prepared raita. Keep raita in the fridge till serving time. Serve cold.

Poodina Raita

Serves 4-5

500 gms yogurt (2½ cups)
¾ cup chopped mint leaves (*poodina*), 1 tsp powdered sugar
1 tbsp raisins (*kishmish*), ½ onion - chopped finely
1 tomato - chopped finely, 1 green chilli - chopped finely, salt and red chilli powder to taste

1. Beat yogurt well, till smooth. Wash mint leaves well and grind to a rough paste.
2. Add all the ingredients to the yogurt. Mix well. Keep in the fridge till serving time.

Dahi Poodina Chutney

Serves 6

GRIND TOGETHER

½ cup mint (*poodina*), ½ cup green coriander
2 green chillies, ½ onion, 2 flakes garlic

ADD LATER

1½ cups yogurt - hang for 15 minutes in a muslin cloth, 1 tsp oil
a pinch of black salt (*kala namak*), ¼ tsp roasted cumin (*bhuna jeera*), salt to taste

1. Wash coriander and mint leaves.
2. Grind coriander, mint, green chillies, onion and garlic with a little water to a paste.
3. Beat yogurt well till smooth.
4. To the hung yogurt, add green paste, oil, black salt, roasted cumin and salt. Mix.

Instant Khatti Mithi Chutney

Serves 6

1 tbsp dry mango powder (*amchoor*), 3 tbsp sugar or shakkar (*gur*)
½ tsp roasted cumin seeds (*jeera*), ¼ tsp red chilli powder, ¼ tsp salt, ¼ tsp garam masala

1. Mix all ingredients together in a small heavy bottomed pan with ¼ cup of water.
2. Cook on low flame, till all the ingredients dissolve properly and the chutney gets the right consistency. Remove from fire.

Chilli Garlic Chutney

Serves 8

4-5 dry red chillies - deseeded and soaked in ¼ cup water, 6-8 flakes garlic
1 tsp coriander seeds (*saboot dhania*), 1 tsp cumin seeds (*jeera*), 1 tbsp oil
½ tsp salt, 1 tsp sugar, 3 tbsp vinegar

1. For the chutney, grind the soaked chillies along with the water, garlic, coriander seeds, cumin seeds, oil and sugar and vinegar to a paste.

Tomato Chutney

A sweet and hot, South Indian tomato chutney.

Serves 8-10

4 large tomatoes - chopped finely, ¼ cup water
½ tsp salt or to taste
1 tsp sambhar powder, a tiny pieces of jaggery (*gur*)

TEMPERING (CHOWNK)
1 tbsp oil, ½ tsp mustard seeds (*sarson*)
a pinch of asafoetida (*hing*) powder, a few curry leaves - chopped, ½ tsp red chilli powder

1. Heat oil in a heavy bottomed pan. Reduce flame and add sarson and hing.
2. When it splutters, after ½ minute, add chopped curry leaves and red chilli powder.
3. Add tomatoes. Mix. Add salt. Mash tomatoes for 2-3 minutes.
4. Add water. Simmer, covered, on low flame for 10 minutes. Cook, mashing occasionally, till thick and pulpy.
5. Add sambhar powder and jaggery. Mix well. Remove from fire after a few minutes.
6. Serve with rice, idlis or dosas.

Coconut Chutney

Fresh coconut is traditional, but to make the procedure simpler, you may opt for the desiccated coconut instead.

Serves 4

½ cup freshly grated or desiccated coconut
½ cup roasted peanuts (without the red skin)
1 green chilli - chopped, 1 onion - chopped (½ cup)
½ tsp salt, or to taste, ½ inch/1 cm piece ginger
1 cup yogurt

TEMPERING
1 tsp mustard seeds (*sarson*)
1-2 dry, red chillies - broken into bits, a few curry leaves

1. Grind all ingredients of the chutney adding enough yogurt to get a thick paste of soft dropping consistency. Keep aside in a bowl.
2. To temper the chutney, heat 1 tbsp oil. Add mustard seeds. When they splutter, add broken red chillies and curry leaves. Remove from heat and pour the tempered oil on the chutney. Mix lightly.

Sweet Dishes

sweet dishes

Moong Dal Payasam

The secret is to carefully dry-roast the dal before using it. Taste the best of Kerala's beautiful cuisine in this famous dessert made with moong dal, milk, jaggery, coconut milk and cashew nuts.

Serves 6

¾ cup yellow moong dal
2¼ cups water
1 cup grated or powdered jaggery (*gur*), or to taste
seeds of 8 green cardamoms (*chhoti elaichi*) - powdered
a few cashew nuts (*kaju*) - broken into pieces, ¾ cup milk, 1 cup coconut milk
a few raisins, a small piece coconut - peeled into thin slices with a peeler
1 tbsp ghee

1. Dry roast dal in a kadhai to a light brown colour for about 5 minutes till it gives out a nice smell. Remove from kadhai and let it cool. Wash the dal.

2. Put dal in a pressure cooker. Add water and pressure cook to give 4 whistles or keep on low heat for 3-4 minutes after the pressure forms. Remove from heat and let the pressure drop.

3. Open the cooker and keep on low heat. Mash the cooked dal with a kadchi till almost smooth. Add jaggery and cook on low heat till jaggery dissolves.

4. Add milk and coconut milk, simmer further for 2-3 minutes. Remove the payasam from heat. Check sweetness.

5. Add cardamom powder. Mix.

6. Heat 1 tbsp ghee, fry cashew nut pieces, coconut pieces and raisins, each separately. Add these to the payasam.

Badam Paan

Badam dough is rolled out and divided into triangles. Each triangle is stuffed with a traditional 'meetha paan' filling, enclosed to look like a 'paan', and neatly studded with a clove.

Makes 7

BADAM COVERING
½ cup almonds - blanched, peeled and dried, 1 tbsp milk powder
¼ cup sugar, 1/8 cup water

FILLING
1 tbsp gulukand
1 tbsp soft mithi supari - crushed lightly in a grinder
1½ tbsp khoya, 2 almonds, 2 kaju and 2 pista - all chopped

TOPPING
a few cloves (*laung*), silver sheet (*varak*)

1. Soak almonds in hot water for 1 hour. Peel skin and dry under a fan. Grind finely in a nicely dried grinder. (There should be no moisture or water in the grinder). The almonds do not remain a powder but turn into a fine paste because of the oil in the almonds. Keep aside.

2. In a medium flat non stick pan, put sugar and water and stir frequently till sugar dissolves. Cook further on low heat for about 3-4 minutes to get a one thread consistency syrup.

3. Remove syrup from fire. Add ground almonds and milk powder to the hot syrup and mix well. Keep stirring briskly with a wooden spoon for about 2-3 minutes. The mixture leaves the sides of the pan as you keep stirring and starts collecting like a ball in the pan. Remove from pan and keep aside for the mixture to cool for 5 minutes.

4. Cover almond dough and keep aside.

5. For filling, mix all ingredients. Keep aside.

6. Roll the almond ball like a chappati on a plastic sheet to a round of about 8" diameter.

7. Cut the circle into half.

8. Divide each half into 3 triangles to get 6 triangles in all. Each triangle will be with one side curved.

9. Trim the curved side to get a proper triangle.

10. Hold two corners slightly overlapping the sides, to form a cone. Press the joint lightly.

11. Put some filling in the cone.

12. Cover the filling with the remaining portion of the almond dough to get a neat triangle. Press lightly to seal. Turn paan and apply silver varak. Insert a clove in the centre. Make one paan from the trimmings also.

Illustrated reference from Steps 6-10

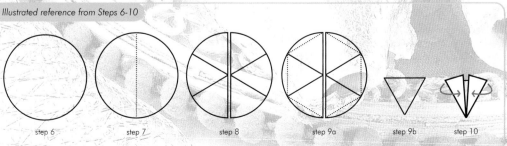

step 6   step 7   step 8   step 9a   step 9b   step 10

Makhane ki Kheer

Indian cuisine uses some very exotic ingredients such as lotus seeds. In this recipe they are first roasted then simmered in sweetened milk to make a very special and unique dessert.

Serves 8

2 kg milk
100 gms puffed lotus seeds (*makhane*) - roast for 1-2 minutes in a pan
¾ cup sugar or to taste, ½ tsp green cardamom (*chhoti elaichi*) powder
2-3 tbsp screwpine flower (*kewra*) water
1 tbsp chopped green pistachios, 2-3 sheets silver leaf (*vark*)

1. Roast the puffed lotus seeds till they start to change colour. Let them cool. Crush half of them, leaving the other whole.

2. Boil milk. When the milk starts to boil, add the lotus seeds and cook on medium heat, stirring every now and then. Cook till the lotus seeds are cooked and the consistency of the milk reduced by one third.

3. Add sugar and sprinkle crushed cardamom. Continue cooking for a couple of minutes. Remove from heat.

4. Add kewra water. Transfer the kheer to a serving dish. Decorate with vark and chopped pistachios.

NOTE:

½ cup freshly grated coconut can be added after removing the kheer from heat to get makhane aur nariyal ki kheer.

Mango Kulfi

Makes 8

1 large mango - chopped (1½ cups), 6½ cups milk
7 tbsp sugar, seeds of 3-4 green cardamom - crushed
2 tbsp cornflour mixed with ½ cup milk
8-10 pistachios (*pistas*) - blanched and chopped
½ cup fresh cream

1. Keeping ½ cup chopped mango aside, puree the rest of the mango (1 cup) with ½ cup milk in a mixer.
2. Boil 6 cups milk with sugar & green cardamom for about 20 minutes on low heat till it is reduced to about ½ quantity, about 3 cups.
3. Add cornflour paste stirring continuously. Stir for 5 minutes on low heat. Remove from fire and let the milk cool.
4. Add mango puree to thickened milk. Mix well. Add finely chopped mango pieces and finely chopped pistachios also.
5. Add cream. Mix well. Pour into *kulfi* moulds and freeze for 5-6 hours or overnight.

Kesari Shrikhand

*The thick & creamy texture of drained & sweetened yogurt makes every mouthful a luscious
pleasure. The subtle touches of cardamom, nutmeg & saffron heighten the enjoyment.*

Serves 6

1 kg yogurt (thick and fresh) of full cream milk
1 cup (150 gms) sugar - powdered
¼ tsp saffron (*kesar*) - soaked in 1 tbsp warm milk for 5 minutes
½ tsp green cardamom (*chhoti elaichi*) powder, ¼ tsp nutmeg (*jaiphal*) powder
2 tbsp cream, 4-5 almonds (*badam*) and 4-5 pistachios (*pista*) - sliced

1. Tie the freshly set yogurt in a muslin cloth for 3-4 hours. In summers you can tie it in the
    fridge and keep an empty bowl beneath it to collect the liquid.
2. Pass this yogurt through a sieve (soup strainer) to make it smooth.
3. Add powdered sugar, cardamom, nutmeg, saffron, cream and mix well. Transfer to a
    serving bowl.
4. Garnish with saffron, sliced almonds and pistachios. Serve cold.

International Conversion Guide

These are not exact equivalents; they've been rounded-off to make measuring easier.

WEIGHTS & MEASURES

METRIC	IMPERIAL
15 g	½ oz
30 g	1 oz
60 g	2 oz
90 g	3 oz
125 g	4 oz (¼ lb)
155 g	5 oz
185 g	6 oz
220 g	7 oz
250 g	8 oz (½ lb)
280 g	9 oz
315 g	10 oz
345 g	11 oz
375 g	12 oz (¾ lb)
410 g	13 oz
440 g	14 oz
470 g	15 oz
500 g	16 oz (1 lb)
750 g	24 oz (1 ½ lb)
1 kg	30 oz (2 lb)

LIQUID MEASURES

METRIC	IMPERIAL
30 ml	1 fluid oz
60 ml	2 fluid oz
100 ml	3 fluid oz
125 ml	4 fluid oz
150 ml	5 fluid oz (¼ pint/1 gill)
190 ml	6 fluid oz
250 ml	8 fluid oz
300 ml	10 fluid oz (½ pint)
500 ml	16 fluid oz
600 ml	20 fluid oz (1 pint)
1000 ml	1¾ pints

CUPS & SPOON MEASURES

METRIC	IMPERIAL
1 ml	¼ tsp
2 ml	½ tsp
5 ml	1 tsp
15 ml	1 tbsp
60 ml	¼ cup
125 ml	½ cup
250 ml	1 cup

HELPFUL MEASURES

METRIC	IMPERIAL
3 mm	1/8 in
6 mm	¼ in
1 cm	½ in
2 cm	¾ in
2.5 cm	1 in
5 cm	2 in
6 cm	2½ in
8 cm	3 in
10 cm	4 in
13 cm	5 in
15 cm	6 in
18 cm	7 in
20 cm	8 in
23 cm	9 in
25 cm	10 in
28 cm	11 in
30 cm	12 in (1 ft)

HOW TO MEASURE

When using the graduated metric measuring cups, it is important to shake the dry ingredients loosely into the required cup. Do not tap the cup on the table, or pack the ingredients into the cup unless otherwise directed. Level top of cup with a knife. When using graduated metric measuring spoons, level top of spoon with a knife. When measuring liquids in the jug, place jug on a flat surface, check for accuracy at eye level.

OVEN TEMPERATURE

These oven temperatures are only a guide. Always check the manufacturer's manual.

	°C *(Celsius)*	°F *(Fahrenheit)*	Gas Mark
Very Low	120	250	1
Low	150	300	2
Moderately Low	160	325	3
Moderate	180	350	4
Moderately High	190	375	5
High	200	400	6
Very High	230	450	7

Glossary

Hindi or English Names used in India	As English names as used in USA/UK/ Other Countries	Hindi or English Names used in India	As English names as used in USA/UK/ Other Countries
Aloo	Potatoes	Kofta	Balls made from minced vegetables or meat, fried and put in a curry/gravy/sauce.
Badaam	Almonds		
Baingan	Eggplant, aubergine		
Basmati rice	Fragrant Indian rice	Maida	All purpose flour, Plain flour
Bhutta	Corn	Makai, Makki	Corn
Bhindi	Okra, ladys finger	Makhan	Butter
Capsicum	Bell peppers	Matar	Peas
Chaawal, Chawal	Rice	Mitha soda	Baking soda
Chhoti Illaichi	Green cardamom	Nimbu	Lemon
Chilli powder	Red chilli powder, Cayenne pepper	Paneer	Home made cheese made by yogurtling milk with vinegar or lemon juice. Fresh home made ricotta cheese can be substituted.
Cornflour	Cornstarch		
Coriander, fresh	Cilantro		
Cream	Heavy whipping cream	Patta Gobhi	Cabbage
Dalchini	Cinnamon	Phalli	Green beans
French beans	Green beans	Powdered sugar	Castor sugar
Gajar	Carrots	Pyaz, pyaaz	Onions
Gobhi	Cauliflower	Red Capsicum	Red bell peppers
Hara Dhania	Cilantro/fresh or green coriander	Red chilli flakes	Red pepper flakes
		Saboot Kali mirch	Peppercorns
Hari Gobhi	Broccoli	Saunf	Fennel
Hari Mirch	Green hot peppers, green chillies, serrano peppers	Sela Chaawal	Parboiled rice, which when cooked is not sticky at all
Illaichi	Cardamom		
Imli	Tamarind	Seviyaan	Vermicelli
Jeera Powder	Ground cumin seeds	Shimla Mirch	Green bell peppers
Kadhai/Karahi	Wok	Soda bicarb	Baking soda
Kaju	Cashewnuts	Spring Onions	Green onions, Scallions
Katori	Individual serving bowls resembling ramekins	Suji	Semolina
		Tamatar	Tomato
Khumb	Mushrooms	Til	Sesame seeds
Kishmish	Raisins	Toned Milk	Milk with 1% fat content
		Yellow Capsicum	Yellow bell peppers
		Zeera	Cumin seeds

BEST SELLING COOKBOOKS BY

SNAB
Excellence in Books

Cookbook of Rajasthan

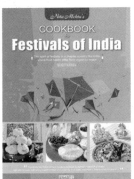
Cookbook for Festivals of India

101 Recipes for Children

Permanent Weight Loss Cookbook

Indian Cooking with Olive Oil

Traditional & Innovative MITHAI

Learn to Cook Chinese - Vegetarian

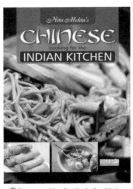
Chinese cooking for the Indian kitchen

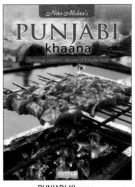
PUNJABI Khaana

101 Chicken Recipes

Tandoori cooking in the Microwave & Oven

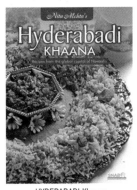
HYDERABADI Khaana

Eggless Cakes & Muffins

Microwave Desi Khaana

101 Microwave Recipes

101 Diet Recipes

Tell me about MAHABHARATA

101 Tales from Indian Mythology

Tell me about KRISHNA

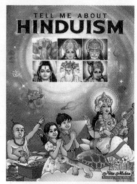

Tell me about HINDUISM

Tell me about HANUMAN

Tell me about GANESHA

Tell me about SIKH GURUS

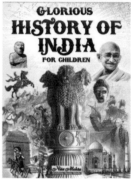

Glorious HISTORY of INDIA

Tales of KRISHNA

Tales of GODS & DEMONS

Tales from ARABIA

Tales of WISDOM from India

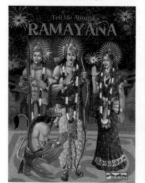

Tell me about RAMAYANA

ANCIENT Tales

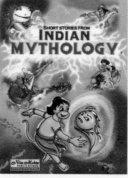

Short stories from INDIAN MYTHOLOGY

Great Stories for Children Vol. I to 10.